BROADER NORFOLK

Bishy-Barny bee

BROADER
NORFOLK

Being a
quizzical
investigation
into the
exceptional dialect,
places and
characteristics
of the
County of Norfolk
as collected by

David Stannard

and illustrated
by the pen of

George Smith

The Larks Press

Published by the Larks Press
Ordnance Farmhouse, Guist Bottom
Dereham NR20 5PF
01328 829207
E-mail: Larks.Press@btinternet.com

Website: www.booksatlarkspress.co.uk

Printed by the Lanceni Press, Garrood Drive, Fakenham

British Cataloguing-in-publication Data
A catalogue record for this book is available from the British Library

To the memory of G.C.S.

ISBN 1 904006 03 5

Contents

Foreword

'Every one has heard of the Norfolk "drant" or droning and
drawling in speech'.
*'On Early English Pronunciation with special reference to
Shakespeare and Chaucer' A. J. Ellis (1869-89)*

When the Reverend Robert Forby produced *The Vocabulary of East Anglia*
(published posthumously in 1830) he expressed concern that the unique
native language of the eastern counties was soon to be lost forever. Just about
everybody else who has produced works on the Norfolk dialect has said much
the same thing. They suggest that the influence of 'the outside world' upon
the good people of Norfolk inevitably dilutes the uniqueness of the language
and narrows the vocabulary to a few quaint words and phrases of rural
insignificance.

I would maintain that this simply isn't true. This book, in a small way,
tries to dispel the myth that the distinctiveness of the Norfolk dialect is being
lost in the 'communication society' of the twenty-first century and that the
concept we call 'globalisation' is the evil driving force behind this supposed
loss.

Through the 1950s Potter Heigham resident, Sidney Grapes (1888-1958)
in the guise of 'The Boy John', raised the standard of Norfolk's dialectical
genius in a wonderful series of letters which fell, unannounced and as warmly
welcomed as manna from Heaven, on the desk of the Editor of the *Eastern
Daily Press*. To popular acclaim, these letters, which described the comings
and goings of the life of a Norfolk family and their village, appeared
intermittently over nearly a decade in the pages of that newspaper. The torch
that The Boy John so cleverly kindled has flickered in the cold east wind of
the intervening years, but its light has been carried by others and has never
died.

Happily, I am pleased to report that Norfolk's distinctive words, phrases
and place-names are as commonly used now as they ever were, held in trust
by a collective folk memory that is strong and active. The creation of a
Norfolk Dialect Society in 1999 demonstrates that there is indeed an abiding
desire to maintain and enrich this distinctive form of communication for those
who are willing to look for, and listen to its distinctive sounds and unique
modulation.

But this is not to say that 'Norfolkisms' haven't changed over time.
Language and dialect are the most moveable of moveable feasts, and we
Norfolk dialecticians must be careful to recognise the difference between
preservation and conservation; the latter is a cultural celebration of heritage
whilst the former, to the unwary, can be the road to rigid self-destruction.

And what of these foreign invaders intent on demeaning the rich culture of Norfolk and changing its language for all time?

Well, the more I probed and dissected this Norfolk dialect the more I discovered that it is these very changes, and these very people, that have created the singular phenomenon which we call 'broad Norfolk'. Here is a process which I believe is something to be encouraged and recognised for what it is, an enrichment of our heritage.

To be of Norfolk is to be of the *Ikenny*, those eastern Iron Age Britons who challenged and then absorbed the best, and the worst, of Roman influence in the early centuries of the first millenium. To be of Norfolk is to be an East Anglian, speaking the Anglo-Saxon language, which was to become both English and Norfolk; later modified by the Scandinavians who ruled eleventh century Norwich and exercised the Danelaw throughout northern and eastern Britain.

To be Norfolk is to use the language of the Normans who recognised, conquered and further enhanced the riches of medieval Norfolk leaving a fabulous legacy of castles, cathedrals, ideas and words. Words and structures of language current in Norfolk today were brought by seventeenth century Walloon and Flemish immigrants fleeing persecution, and the 'invasion' of North American nationals to Great Yarmouth in the 1960s, searching for North Sea oil and gas, created more than just 'Yarmouth Yanks'; their lusty presence will forever linger in our language.

This book takes a less than traditional approach to dialect and is compiled as a series of quizzes intended to celebrate, inform and most of all to prompt further inquiry into what Norfolk means to its inhabitants and the rest of the world.

Long may they prosper.

David Stannard
Norfolk
April 2002

Author's Notes

The East Anglian Dialect

Whilst throughout this book the words and phrases examined have been attributed solely to Norfolk, the author must of course acknowledge that the inhabitants of Suffolk, Cambridgeshire and Lincolnshire have every right to regard many of these words as their own. The singular reference to Norfolk has been used merely for the sake of brevity rather than to imply any sense of distinctive ownership.

Foreign Words

All foreign words, by that I mean words which are not current in modern English are italicised as are Latin species names.

Usage

Each dialect word, wherever possible, is accompanied by a quotation showing the way in which the word is or has been used.

Abbreviations

Common abbreviations used in the text are as follows:

AD	Anno domini - in the year of the Lord
BC	Before Christ
Brewer	*The Dictionary of Phrase and Fable* by E. Cobhom Brewer
EDP	Eastern Daily Press
No.	Number
OED	*Oxford English Dictionary*
Forby	Reverend Robert Forby (1732-1825) Rector of Fincham, Norfolk
RNLI	Royal National Lifeboat Institution
US	United States

Scientific Names

All flora and fauna are identified in the text by both their common and scientific Latin names.

Principal Languages

Norfolk dialect has evolved from a number of different languages; the following is a brief guide to the principal languages referred to in the definitions:

Anglo-Saxon	A unified language spoken by the West Germanic people of the same name (comprising Angles, Saxons and Jutes) who settled in Britain from the fifth century. An alternative name for Old English.
British	The language of the ancient Britons before the coming of English. Also known as Celtic or Welsh.
Celtic	A branch of the Indoeuropean family of languages which includes modern Scottish Gaelic, Irish, Welsh and the minor Celtic languages of Cornish and Manx.

Dutch	The modern language of the people of The Netherlands.
Flemish	The Germanic language spoken in Belgium that is almost identical with Dutch.
Frisian	A native of Friesland (northern Netherlands) or their Low German language.
Gaelic	See Celtic
High German	The standard German language of today, derived from Old High German. 'High' refers to the uplands of southern Germany from where the language originated.
Latin	The classical language of the Romans. Low or Vulgar Latin are general terms for non-classical forms of the language. These include Late Latin, the form in use from the third to seventh centuries, Medieval Latin which was used in the Middle Ages, and New Latin which came after the Renaissance (around the sixteenth century). New Latin is used especially for scientific terminology.
Low German	A language of northern (lowland) Germany spoken in rural areas and somewhat closer to Dutch than standard German. (See also Frisian, High German & Old High German).
Middle English	The form of English in general use in the Middle Ages from around 1100AD to 1500AD.
Modern English	The form of English spoken after 1500AD.
Norman French	The medieval Norman and English dialect of Old French (O.F.) (which was in use from 800AD-1400AD), spoken by Normans in England after their invasion of 1066AD.
Old English	The early form of the English language from the fifth century to about 1100AD. Also known as Anglo-Saxon.
Old High German	The language of southern Germany (where the terrain is higher) spoken prior to 1200AD (See also High German & Low German)
Old Norse	The language spoken in Scandinavia from about 700AD to 1350AD. The Vikings (Danes, Norwegians, Swedes) introduced Norse into Britain in the ninth century.
Walloon	Of or pertaining to a people living in southern Belgium and adjoining parts of eastern France; or of their language, a dialect of French.

1. Down in the Marshes

When ninth century Danish settlers started cutting peat for fuel, creating a series of pits in the landscape, they began the process which was to result in the formation of the Broads. Peat-digging continued for several centuries, an early example of industrial despoliation. Subsequent flooding in the thirteenth century filled the pits and created the distinctive Broadland landscape of reed-fringed waters, showing that Mother Nature is always ready to reclaim her own. But nature, in this case, has needed a helping hand, for by late medieval times Dutch drainage engineers were employed to manage and drain Broadland, using an advanced system of windpumps and drainage channels. In doing so they not only created the landscape which we enjoy today, but also introduced into the Norfolk dialect words which describe the tools and techniques used in maintaining this landscape. These words are rarely heard outside East Norfolk, can you answer the following?

1. Where would you find a ligger?
2. How would you use a crome?
3. The tract of land lying to the north of Great Yarmouth is called the Fleggs, but what is a flegg?
4. What is a jet?
5. What is a dydle (didal or didle)?

A ligger across the dyke

Answers

1. Derived from the old Dutch word *legger*, to lie, the word is used in a number of ways in Norfolk. A ligger is a narrow plank laid across a *dyke* (another word of Dutch origin meaning a ditch) which is used as a bridge. We also find a variation of the word used universally by anglers; 'ledgering' is a means of fishing where the weighted tackle *lies* on the river bed. In Arthur Ransome's *The Big Six* the old eel-catcher, Harry Bangate, remembers 'liggering for pike above Potter Heigham' in his youth.

2, A crome is a long-handled rake used to clear weeds from a dyke. The word may also be used as a verb which betrays its Dutch derivation from *krammer* meaning 'to draw out'. Here we have a relict of the influence of the Flemish land-drainage engineers who came to Norfolk in medieval times and did much to create the landscape as we see it today.
   'A sickle to cut with, a didal and crome.
   For draining of ditches that noies [annoys] thee at home.'
   Five Hundred Points of Good Husbandry: Thomas Tusser (1573)

3. Flegg is related to flag, which derives from the Danish word *flaeg*. In Norfolk dialect it is now applied to a cut piece of turf or peat. The word was probably brought to Norfolk in the ninth century when the invading Danes occupied a recently emerged marshy island which they called Flegg. In that treeless landscape, peat was the only source of fuel, and the diggings, which these early settlers made in their exploitation of this resource, later became flooded to form the Broads. Flag is also another name for the Marsh Iris or Yellow Flag *(Iris pseudacorus L)*.
   'Flags, the surface of the earth which they pare off to burn; the upper turf. Norfolk' *South & East Country Words: John Ray (1674)*

4. 'Jet' means 'to throw out a stream of liquid', thus 'a jet' is a bowl-shaped implement to enable you to do this when clearing a dyke. The word is related to 'jettison' and 'jetsam', and comes from the Anglo-French word *jeter*, to throw. It was probably brought to Norfolk by French-speaking Walloons from Flanders.

Crome and jet

5. A didle (or didal) is a scoop or spade-type implement used to clear out the mud in the bottom of a dyke. It may also have a small net attached to help clear weeds. The word may be a shortened form of 'dyke-delve'; both words are of Frisian and Dutch origin.
   'Paid to the didalmen and other labourers for carrying the mud out of the said ditch [of Norwich Castle].' *Chamberlain's Accounts (1490) translated in The History of the Religious Orders and Communities of Norwich: John Kirkpatrick (1845)*

2. Down Your Way

The shape and structure of our Norfolk towns, and the pattern of their streets, have often been created or modified by the needs and practices of trades and occupations in times past. Here are some examples from across the county. Can you explain the derivation of these ancient location names?

1. The Neatherd in Dereham
2. Pottergate in Norwich
3. Norwich Maddermarket
4. Tombland in Norwich
5. The Bleaches in Great Yarmouth

Pottergate c. AD 1000

Answers

1. 'Neat' is an Old English word for cattle, thus a 'neat-herd' is a group of cattle or a person who tends the cattle. The village common land was traditionally used for grazing, and although the modern town of Dereham has now grown up around its common, the name Neatherd, locally pronounced 'netted', survives as a reminder of this activity.

2. Whilst Norwich had twelve medieval gates in its city walls you will not find reference to a 'Potter Gate'. In this case the word ǵate' means a street, and derives from the eleventh century or earlier when Norwich came under the influence of the Danish invaders, the same word is still used for a thoroughfare in Scandinavia today. Pottergate literally means 'the street of the potters', for in 1980 archaeologists excavated a pottery kiln in Bedford Street (historically part of Pottergate) containing earthenware pots which they estimate had been fired about AD1000.

3. & 4. When the Normans came to Norwich soon after the Conquest they created for themselves a French Borough (the *Franci de Norwic*) on agricultural land outside the existing Anglo-Scandinavian town. Political and economic control over the city was ensured by moving the market from Tombland into this new borough in the lee of the great castle which was then being built.
'Tombland, the site of the market place with the place-name meaning an empty or open space.' *Book of Norwich: Brian Ayers (1994)*

Norwich quickly grew in dominance and the streets and lanes in the new market area took on the names of the wares which were sold there. Most important of all to the local economy was the production of worsted cloth, which was dyed using madder *(Rubia tinctorum)* and other plant dyes, often imported from the Norman homelands in Amiens and Corbie. The Maddermarket was where this essential commodity was traded, probably at the bottom of the street running from the market to St Andrew's street.

5. Throughout the centuries the Great Yarmouth herring industry called for the production, washing and maintenance of large numbers of coarse linen (hemp) and later cotton fishing nets. (See pp 17 & 49) The Bleaches (or bleaching grounds) were open areas where linen could be laid out, the work often being undertaken by young children. Gradually these areas became enclosed as paved squares in the very heart of the town; you will find them marked on ancient town maps. Social reformer, Harriet Martineau, knew of the bleachers and the hard work done 'in yonder bleaching ground'. *Harriet Martineau – Vanderput & Son v85 (1833)*
'On Wednesday Yarmouth Mayor David Thompson officially declared the Bleaches [a recently landscaped area behind Camden Road] open, watched by residents.' *Great Yarmouth Mercury Friday August 3 2001*

3. Ancient Hostelries

Traditional pub names are a rich source of social history. This collection looks at some less than obvious examples in the Great Yarmouth area. All of these names are very firmly linked to Yarmouth's maritime traditions, from past glories right up to the present day. Can you say how the names of these ancient hostelries came about?

1. The Barking Smack, Marine Parade, Great Yarmouth
2. The Short Blue, High Street, Gorleston
3. The Red Herring, Havelock Road, Great Yarmouth
4. The Rising Flame, Wolseley Road, Great Yarmouth
5. The Never Turn Back, Caister-on-Sea

Answers

1. In the 1850s Samuel Hewett of Barking, Essex, introduced into the Great Yarmouth area a revolutionary piece of technology which was to establish the town at the forefront of the fishing industry for the next hundred years. This radical development was the 'Barking smack', a sturdy two-masted fishing vessel with a design of hull and 'dandy-rigged' sail pattern (introduced in the 1870s) that was ideally suited to negotiate the local offshore banks and shallows. This pub was the headquarters of the Star Beach Company, one of many nineteenth century east coast co-operatives comprising tough seafarers who secured a precarious living effecting rescues and salvage from shipwrecks and other maritime accidents.

2. Hewett's Short Blue Fleet of Barking smacks, operating from Gorleston, dominated the local fishing industry by introducing the 'fleet method' of fishing. The fishing smacks would stay on the fishing grounds for a number of weeks, transferring their catch to fast cutters in boxes (trunks) packed with ice, and these boats would then race to catch an early market, usually Billingsgate. However, the age of steam was to further revolutionise the industry and the entire fleet of some 115 vessels was laid up in 1899. This pub name is one of the last memories of that glorious age of sail when 'wooden boats were crewed by men of steel'!

3. Salted and heavily-smoked red herrings have been produced in Great Yarmouth since medieval times. It is highly appropriate that a pub should celebrate this traditional product, for as every local publican knows a dish of this aromatic delicacy, toasted on a fork over an open fire, will invoke a powerful thirst which only a well-brewed pint of beer will properly quench!

4. Here we have social history in the making for this pub name celebrates the great industry which replaced the town's traditional fishing industry following the collapse of the herring fishery in the early 1960s. On December 9th 1965 the exploration rig *Sea Gem* announced the first discovery of natural gas in commercially viable quantities in the southern sector of the North Sea. Within a few years much of Great Yarmouth's industry had successfully adapted to meet the maritime and engineering needs of the oil companies which were developing the gas fields, and the sight of rising flames as each new gas discovery was flared, tested and brought on-line became a familiar sight off the Norfolk coast.

5. In 1901 Caister fisherman and retired lifeboatman James Haylett (1824-1907) was asked whether he believed that the *Beauchamp* Lifeboat was giving up in its rescue attempt when it capsized in a tragedy which claimed the lives of several of his relatives. This fine old man's response to Counsel at the official enquiry has passed into folklore. His unswerving claim that Caister men would never turn back inspired the unique name of this pub.

4. Dead as Dodos?

Many of our Norfolk dialect words refer to animals, names which themselves have become extinct in the same way as the poor old Dodo *(sp. Raphidae)*. Several of these are found lurking in literature from across the ages, can you identify these literary references to beasts and birds?

1. *Bill Jenkins, one of the 'Death and Glorys' from Arthur Ransome's Coots in the North*
   'That Dick, he out with his book and write it down when I tell him the other name for a buttle.'
   What is the other name for a buttle? Come to that, what's a buttle?

2. *Shakespeare's Hamlet Act II Scene ii :*
   'I am but mad north-north-west. When the wind is southerly, I know a hawk from a handsaw.'
   What was a handsaw in Hamlet's time ?

3. *Anstey's Bath Guide (1766):*
   'As snug as a hod'mandod rides in his shell.'
   What is a hodmandod?

4. *Norfolk writer Jane Hales in Norfolk Year (1970) :*
   'Then there are the famous Stewkey Blues, besides lesser breeds.'
   What is a Stewkey Blue, and why is it blue?

5. *Sea, land or air; where would you find a kittywitch?*

Answers

1. A 'buttle' is a bittern, *(Botaurus stellaris)* a rare and protected bird species even in the 1930s when Arthur Ransome(1884-1967) wrote his classic children's novels based in Broadland. The name may be a corruption of bottle, from the distinctive shape of the bird with its long neck, or perhaps from its Latin name *botaurus. Coots in the North* was discovered as an unnamed and incomplete Ransome manuscript and not published until 1988.

2. From the Oxford English Dictionary (OED): 'Handsaw is generally explained as a corruption of *heronshaw* or *hernsew,* dialect harnsa. Heron, *(Ardea cinera)* the large grey bird of Broadland.'

3. The 'hodmandod', or 'dodman' is a snail *(Helix aspersa)*. The derivation is from hodman, the man who carries bricks in a hod on his back.

4. The North Norfolk coastal village of Stiffkey boasts the finest cockle *(Cardium edule)* beds in the whole of Norfolk. These wide sandy stretches overlie deposits of thick grey/blue clay, which may be exposed and washed over by the scouring tides. As the cockle grows, it lays down successive layers of calciferous shell, in which thin bands of this clay sediment are entrapped, giving the shell a distinctive blue cast. In Domesday Book Stiffkey is spelt *Stiuekai* from which we get Stewkey, (the name is Old English for Stump Island); hence Stewkey Blues. With the recent recognition of a circle of wooden stumps along the coast at Holme, dubbed by the press 'Seahenge', the name Stump Island may prove to have more significance than first appears.

Stewkey Blue

5. Sea, land or air? – the answer has to be all three!
A Scottish dialect word; the prefix kitty may be applied to a number of animals including a kittiwake *(Rissa tridactyla),* but the OED also defines it in the Norfolk sense as a small swimming crab. These are the pinky-white shore crabs *(Porcellana platycheles)* that are caught when shrimping from the beach. They are distinguished from the common shore crabs by their pair of flat, fringed paddles which enable them to swim. Perhaps the word was brought to Norfolk by the Scottish fisherfolk 'following the fishing'? (See p. 63 for a different land definition of Kittywitch).

5. Give us a Job!

With the advent of the steam drifter at the turn of the century the expansion of the herring fishery in Lowestoft and Yarmouth ensured employment for thousands of East Anglians and visiting Scots. This massive industry created occupations which have now long since disappeared, but the words still linger in our language. How did the following make a living ?

1. *This quote is from an old postcard, depicting the Lowestoft Fishquay, which was written in Beccles on the 16th. July 1909 by Mr.F.E.Chilvers to Tom Adcock, of Camberwell Cottages, Lowestoft.:*
   'Tom, if you want a three-quarter share man I can get one here; netrope or driver. Please let me know.'

   What was a three-quarter share man?

2. *Fisherman Billy Thorpe (born 1908) quoted in The Driftermen by David Butcher (1979):*
   'Well then you had the whaleman...when you landed the herrin' he allus used t'be on the quay with the hawseman and the mate seein t' things there.'

   What were the on-board jobs of a whaleman and hawseman?

3. *A Traditional Yarmouth Shanty quoted in Breeze For A Bargeman by Bob Roberts (1981):*
   'The farmer has his rent to pay, haul you joskins haul,
   And seed to buy I've heard him say, haul you joskins haul.'

   Who or what were joskins ?

4. *Minnie Pitcher (born Lowestoft 1905) is quoted in Following the Fishing by David Butcher:*
   'To be a good beatster, you'd have to do a year's training.'

   What was a beatster?

5. *Flip Garnham (born 1909) quoted in The Driftermen (1979) by David Butcher:*
   'The girls beat the nets and then they're passed to the ransacker'.

   What was a ransacker?

Answers

1. The crew of a herring drifter were paid on a complex profit-share basis, with the major shares going to the owner, skipper and mate of the vessel. Three-quarter share men, deckhands, constituted the bulk of the muscle power on board ship, their principal role being to shoot (cast) and haul anything up to one and a half miles of drift-nets each night. A driver kept the vessel's steam engine operating with the assistance of a stoker.

2. With a rank just below the mate the hawseman and whaleman were the more experienced crew members on a herring drifter who supervised the three-quarter share men. When shooting or hauling the nets their greater experience was needed to operate the system of ropes (hawsers) and winches used for controlling the whole operation. For this work they usually received an extra 'half quarter' (i.e. one eighth) share. 'Hawseman' is undoubtedly short for 'hawser man' but 'whaleman' (or waleman) is more doubtful. Whilst a good indication of the whereabouts of the herring shoals was given by feeding whales ('blowers') whaleman probably derives from 'wale', defined as 'planks along a ship's sides'.

3. The postcard's Beccles postmark confirms that many of the driftermen lived inland, working on the farm for much of the year and moving from the corn harvest to the herring harvest in the Autumn, in order to meet the heavy demands for sheer physical effort that both these activities required. These farm labourers turned fishermen were called 'joskins', yokels by another name. The OED defines 'joskins' as a 'country bumpkin', from joss, to bump.

4. Beatsters were usually females and were employed to beat or repair the cotton drift nets used to catch the herrings. Beat may be spelt *beet* or *bete* and is an Old English word meaning 'to make amends'. The Canterbury Tales give us this description of a talented miller:
      'Pipen he coude and fisshe, and nettes bete,
      And turn coppes, and wel both wrastle and sheete.'
      The Reeves Tale - Geoffrey Chaucer (1340?-1400)

5. A ransacker was a man, usually a foreman, who collected and checked the herring nets for damage. This is an Old Norse word, *rannsaka* means 'to seek or search out' as well as 'plunder and rob'. The meaning may have come directly to Norfolk with the Viking invaders, but it is also known as a Gaelic dialect word and was perhaps introduced by the Scots fisherfolk when they followed the shoals of herring to the east coast every autumn.

6. Just Messing About on the River

In past times the waterways of Broadland were the major trading highways of Norfolk; much of the county's prosperity relied on the trading wherry for the transport of bulk materials. The coming of the railways had an adverse impact on wherry trading, but its death knell was sounded by the rise of motor transport in the early part of the twentieth century. Writing in the late 1930s Arthur Ransome (1884-1967) was a witness to these and other changes in Broadland. As a pioneer environmentalist he chose to deliver his deceptively simple conservation message in the form of superb children's novels, two of which are set firmly in the heart of the Broads at Horning. The following is from one of these novels, *Coot Club*.

'Jim Woodall had indeed been in a hurry, to start quanting his wherry round to the staithe to look for his mate.' *Coot Club* by Arthur Ransome (1936)

Can you identify the source and meaning of the following words which are peculiar to Norfolk ?

1. A wherry?
2. A quant?
3. A staithe?
4. A rond....
5....and why are they called Broads?

Wherry and quant 'when the wind fails'

Answers

1. 'A wherry on the East Norfolk and East Suffolk rivers it is a large sailing boat, carrying from 15 to 35 tons of merchandise.'
Dictionary of Obsolete and Provincial English -Thomas Wright (1857)
Wherry, or *whurry*, is related to *whirr* a rapid movement, but the origin of the word, according to the Oxford English Dictionary, is obscure.

2. A 'quant' comes from an adaptation of the Latin word *contus*, a boat pole. References can be found in medieval Latin manuscripts but this quote from George Christopher Davies (1849-1922), 'the man who found The Broads', says it all:
'When the wind fails the men betake themselves to "the quant", which is a long pole with a knob at one end and a spike and shoulder at the other.'
Norfolk Broads and Rivers – G.C. Davies (1883)

3. A staithe is a landing stage, a meaning which the OED says is 'not evidenced in Old English and is current only in districts where Scandinavian influence is strong.' The fishing village of Staithes is located on the Yorkshire coast which suffered Viking invasion in the same way as East Anglia.

4. A 'rond' (or 'rand') is defined by the Oxford English Dictionary as:
'In East Anglia a marshy reed-covered strip of land lying between the natural river-bank and the artificial embankment.'
Rand is a German and Dutch word for bank, beach, field border, brink, rim, etc. In the village of Hoveton, an important Broadland boating centre, 'The Rhond' appears as the name of a thoroughfare alongside the river.

5. It was only in the 1960s, after painstaking research, that the medieval man-made origin of the Broads was discovered by a team of researchers led by Dr Joyce Lambert. This pioneering work revealed that they are ancient abandoned peat cuttings, cut in the valley bottoms adjacent to the main rivers and subsequently flooded due to a rise in sea level. The OED defines 'broad', a word of Dutch origin, as:
'In East Anglia, an extensive piece of fresh water formed by the 'broadening' out of a river'.

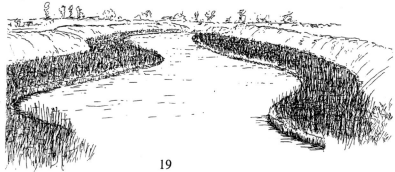

Ronds on either side of a Broad-land river

7. High Sprites

Most country regions have any number of local myths and legends and East Anglia is particularly well represented in this field. Can you identify the origins or activities of the following mythical figures, or 'high sprites' as they are called in Norfolk?

1. Black Shuck
2. Jack Valentine
3. Wood-Wose
4. The Hempstead Seer
5. ...and why are they called High Sprites?

Happisburgh font

Answers

1. Black Shuck is an enormous dog, a hell hound, which if seen on his nocturnal wanderings will bring death to the unfortunate witness within the year. The word comes from Old English *scucca*, a devil or fiend. Lurid stories of Black Shuck undoubtedly helped to shield the activities of coastal smugglers on a dark night; a notorious sunken trackway at Northrepps leads inland from the coast and bears the name Shuck's Lane.

2. Jack Valentine traditionally only appears on the evening of St. Valentine's day (February 14th); he is never seen and his presence is only recognised by a loud knocking on the door. Anyone answering the door may be fortunate enough to find a present has mysteriously appeared on the doorstep, but sometimes there will be nothing at all. This benevolent, but mischievous, mystery man is largely unknown outside Norfolk.
   'Acors we orl got Walentens at nite. Furst cum an ounce o' baccer for Granfar, then two mittens for me... Arter that there cum a tin o' pork for Aunt Agatha. (We sent that). Acors the last lot wot cum wus the brume a fallen in; we new that wus the finish.'
   The Boy John Letters by Sidney Grapes (February 22nd. 1951)

3. A wood-wose, or woodhouse is a wild man of the woods, a green man. These mythical figures are lingering symbols of our pagan past representing belief in the power of mother nature, beliefs which were adopted and translated into Christian doctrine over the ensuing centuries. There are several Green Man pubs in Norfolk, and the leaf-clad faces of wood-wose are often to be found carved in stone or wood in Norfolk churches. Some do say that on occasions the wood-wose climb down from the font in Happisburgh Church and may be seen dancing at the altar!

4. Renowned for his second sight, the publican of the Royal Sovereign at Hempstead, near Stalham, at first refused to cast the fortune of the local squire's drunken and negligent kennel-man. When pressed however, the seer revealed that the kennel-man would die within the month and never be buried. Few mourned as the prophesy came true. When the incompetent wretch eventually deigned to see to his charges he was set upon by his own hungry hounds, who promptly devoured him!
   'His awful fate naturally increased the fame and fear of the Hempstead Seer.' *W.H.Cooke -Manuscript: The Destruction of Eccles-next-the Sea. (1914)*

5. The word sprite comes from the Old French word *esprit* meaning 'spirit' in its various senses, and is perhaps another example of Walloon French influencing our language. As to the reason why they are *high* spirits in Norfolk, unfortunately this still remains obscure.

8. Where Did You Say You Were From?

The rivalry which exists between nearby communities is reflected today in the highs and lows of local Derbys, notably here in East Anglia between Norwich City and Ipswich Town football clubs. In earlier times, the relative isolation of Norfolk meant that this rivalry was even more localised, often from one market town or village to the next. In a rural economy, where farming or fishing were ever subject to the vagaries of the wind and weather this competitive spirit was seen as a necessary adjunct to an often precarious life. The following nicknames, mostly slightly derogatory, all refer to the occupants of Norfolk towns and villages, can you say where and why?

1. A Yarco
2. A Crab
3. A Shannock
4. A Duff-choker
5. A Know-all
6. A Redneck

A 'Cromer Crab'
repairs his pots

Answers

1. A Yarco is someone from Great Yarmouth; the name derives from a firm of ship's chandlers, the Yarmouth Stores Company. The distinctive blue fishermen's smocks which they manufactured instantly identified the wearer as a Yarmouth man throughout the fishing world.
'The Yarmouth men always wore blue ones..."There's an old Yarco", you used t'say.' *George Stock quoted in The Driftermen by David Butcher (1979)*

2. Cromer crabs *(Cancer pagurus)* enjoy a national culinary reputation, so inevitably the residents of this coastal fishing town are called crabs.
'Cromer crabs, Runton dabs,
Beeston babies, Sheringham ladies'
Part of a traditional rhyme quoted by Jonathan Mardle in Broad Norfolk (1973)

3. The fishermen of Sheringham exploit the local crab fishery just as effectively as Cromer men, the long-held rivalry between the two towns calls for a clear distinction in all matters, thus Sheringham residents are traditionally called Shannocks. 'Shanny' (or 'shandy') is a Norfolk word meaning shatter-brained *(Forby's Vocabulary)* and is often applied to precocious young girls. Forby also cites 'shandy' as the harum scarum hero of Laurence Sterne's *Tristram Shandy*. However, none of these is a really satisfactory explanation. I think the jury is still out on this one!

4. Staple fare for the crew of a herring drifter was sweet or savoury suet pudding, known locally as suet duff (a corruption of dough). Hence 'duff-choker' was simply a mildly derogatory term applied to an east coast fisherman, usually from Gt. Yarmouth.
'When you were cook you used t' make yuh light duff. The men used t' like that.' *George Stock of Pakefield quoted in The Driftermen by David Butcher*

5. The residents of Holt are ironically termed 'know-alls', implying they actually know very little!. Since *an owl* (get it?) is featured on the town sign one presumes that the townsfolk bear this slight on their character with some stoicism. A story is told of a captured owl which was placed in an animal pen with an open top, from which the bird promptly escaped.
'The people from Holt were once known as The Holt Knowers (or Know-alls).' *Norfolk Ghosts & Legends - Polly Howat (1993)*

6. 'Redneck' is another nickname for a Yarmouth man implying a lack of culture or learning. It refers to the tanning effect which both wind and sun have on someone who spends a working life exposed to the elements. The term was lost to Norfolk for much of the twentieth century, but was brought back by expatriate Americans working in the oil and gas industry.
'Yarmouth fishermen were known as rednecks or duff-chokers.'
The Driftermen - David Butcher (1979)

9. Ancient Britons

All of the following words have their root in Iceni, the name of the tribe of Iron Age people who lived in Norfolk and witnessed, suffered and ultimately resisted the Roman invasion, eventually integrating with the invaders and forming a society of Romano-British farmers and traders. We know their name from discoveries of coins and ancient manuscripts, whilst their distinctive horse symbol has today been adopted by the Norfolk Museums Service as a logo. The influence of these remarkable early Britons still reaches out over some two thousand years to touch our daily lives as we drive their ancient routes (i.e. the A140 from Norwich to Ipswich) and recognise their ancient wisdoms. Can you identify the location and meaning of:

1. Venta Icenorum (3 miles south of Norwich)
2. The Icknield Way (West Norfolk)
3. Icklingham, Suffolk (5 miles north-east of Bury St Edmunds)
4. The Ikenny
5. Cenomanni or Cenimagni

A coin of the Iceni

Answers

1. *Venta Icenorum* is the name of the provincial capital built to subjugate the Iceni after Boudicca's rebellion; it is a remarkable planned Roman town located at Caistor St. Edmund just to the south of Norwich. The Antonine Itinerary, a contemporary gazetteer of routes of the fourth century Roman Empire, records *Icinos* as an alternative name for *Venta Icenorum*. Recent work has revealed the likely presence of an amphitheatre within the ancient third century walls.

2. This ancient trackway, it is suggested, derived its name from the Iceni; however, it undoubtedly pre-dates the Iceni/Roman period. It may have had its origins in animal migration routes, perhaps around 8000 BC, which developed over hundreds of years into trading routes. This corridor of straggling paths which followed the chalk ridge from the Norfok coast near Hunstanton to Thetford and Newmarket (and probably ran all the way to Wiltshire) was adapted and straightened by the Romans. The track in the Midlands known as Ryknield Street also takes its name from the Icknield Way.

3. The site of the Roman-British villa at Icklingham, a few miles north-west of Bury St Edmunds, lies on the Icknield Way. It was here that archaeologists discovered some of the earliest evidence of practising Christians to be found in this country. This includes two lead baptismal tanks decorated with the chi-rho symbol. Opinion is divided on the name's origin; some scholars link the name of this important site to the Iceni, others to Icel (or Yccel), a fifth century descendant of King Offa the Great.

4. 'Norfolk people were referred to as 'Ikenny' as late as the 1950s'
   Norfolk Origins 2: Roads and Tracks - Bruce Robinson & Edwin Rose (1983)
   There are good reasons for believing that *Iceni* should be pronounced with a hard 'c', so this is presumably a different spelling of the same word.

5. Brewer's *Dictionary of Phrase and Fable* defines *Cenomanni* as 'the inhabitants of Norfolk, Suffolk and Cambridge; referred to by Caesar in his commentaries.'
   Similarly, Dr Tom Williamson of the University of East Anglia writes:
   'Caesar relates how the Trinovantes [in 54 BC], a tribe occupying Essex and much of Suffolk, sought his protection, and how soon afterwards "several other tribes sent emissaries and surrendered, including a group called the *Cenimagni*", presumably a rendering of the name *Iceni*.'
   Origins of Norfolk - Tom Williamson (1993)

10. Standards That Have Slipped

The stand taken by some folk in resisting conversion of our common weights and measures to a metric system reflects a laudable attachment to the familiar, but perhaps fails to recognise that the way in which we measure our world is constantly changing. These changes are driven by need and convenience, and our local dialect abounds with obsolete terms which we have abandoned as circumstance dictates, a process which is still going on today. All these words come from the fishing industry; can you say what, and how much is defined by

1. A mease (or maise)
2. A cran
3. A swill
4. A last
5. A kit

Crans and swills on Yarmouth quay

Answers

1. A 'mease' is a measure of five 'hundred' herring; the word comes from the Old French word *meise,* a box or receptacle. On Yarmouth quay a 'hundred', or more precisely a 'long hundred' of herring comprised 120 fish. This early system of measurement was adopted to account for the variations in size and weight of the individual fish.

2. A 'cran' is also a measure for herring, in this case defined by capacity and fixed by the Board of Fisheries in 1852 at 37½ gallon (equivalent to 28 stone, approximately 1000 fish). Half and quarter-cran wicker baskets, carefully made to the correct dimensions, were used when landing the fish in port. The word is of Scottish origin from the Gaelic *crann,* meaning an allotment or share of fish.
'With the swills you'd start at the top of the basket and work downwards, but with the quarter-crans that was the other way about.' *Stanley Bird - Basketmaker Gt Yarmouth (1987)*

3. 'Swills', the distinctively-shaped boat-like wicker baskets with a central carrying handle were uniquely used in Yarmouth to carry herring (about two thirds of a cran), but were not generally used as a standard measure. Swill comes from the Gaelic *suil,* a willow.
'At Yarmouth the fish are landed in convenient and quaintly shaped baskets called "swills".' *Household Words Vol VI (1853)*

4. 'Last' is a commercial denomination of weight, capacity or quantity applied to a variety of merchandise including barrels of beer, pitch, salt cod, pilchard or herring. The OED says that originally the 'last' must have been the quantity carried at one time by the vehicle (boat, wagon etc.) used for these goods, estimated at something over two tons. The word is from the Old English *hlaest,* related to Old Norse *hlass,* meaning a load.
'A Yarmouth last of herrings is supposed to count 13,200 fish.' *British Almanac and Companion (1884)*

5. A 'kit', defined as ten stone of fish* or the container holding this quantity, was until very recently the commonly used measure for wholesale fresh fish in UK fishing ports. The need to sell fish in Continental markets has caused this 'kit-trade', to be rapidly superseded by measures based on the kilogram. The word comes from the Middle Dutch *kitte,* meaning a wooden vessel made of hooped staves.

   *Not, please note, ten *stones of fishes.* The Norfolk dialect follows the Flemish language which does not usually require the addition of 's' or 'es' to pluralise a word, especially in reference to animals; a convention which survives in English with words such as 'sheep' and 'deer'.

11. To Boldly Go!

Ernest Suffling's boating and tourist guides to Norfolk did much to popularise the county for those Victorian travellers keen to explore these strange and wild regions. His writings provide us with a rich source of information on the distinctive culture and customs of the county. Suffling, who lived in Happisburgh, quotes local farmer Seiley with the following:

'Then, in the night, my ould dickey got over th' deek and fall inter the holl in Cubitt's pightle, and thair she lay till th' mornin.'
The Land of the Broads - Ernest Suffling (c1880)

What exactly is:

1. A dickey (or dicker)?
2. A deek?
3. A holl?
4. A pightle?

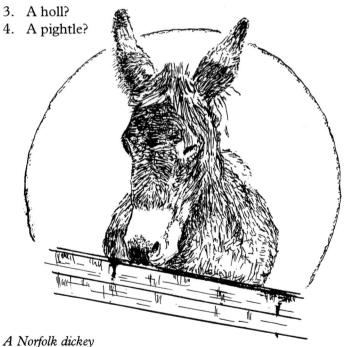

A Norfolk dickey

Answers

1. A 'dickey' is a donkey in Norfolk; the Oxford English Dictionary (OED) says this was 'first noted in East Anglia and Essex, now widely known'. In Robert Bloomfield's *Rural Tales* (1802) we find this reference to a donkey derby:
    'Time to begin the dickey races, more fam'd for laughter than for speed.'

2. 'Deek' is a dialect corruption of the Dutch word *dike,* (or *dyke)* 'a ridge or embankment thrown up to resist the encroachments of the sea'. The Old English word *dic* has given us dike and also ditch; the OED explains that the former means a bank or mound, the latter a hollow to contain water. The two words are interchangeable, perhaps because the action of forming one inevitably produces the other. Living in Happisburgh, farmer Seiley would be well familiar with nearby sea banks used to protect land from sea flooding, hence his distinction between 'deek' and 'holl'.

3. A 'holl', an Old English word, is a Norfolk hole, a small depression or hollow. Forby's *Vocabulary of East Anglia (1885)* defines a holl as 'a ditch, particularly a dry one'. This comes from George Baldry's memories of an early traffic accident when the cart in which he is travelling to Lowestoft ends up in the ditch (sorry, I mean holl!):
    'Dang yer tacken', shouts the driver,
    'there's holls both sides 'er
    this 'ere road - keep clear
    of the holls I tells yer!'
    The Rabbit Skin Cap –
    George Baldry (1939)

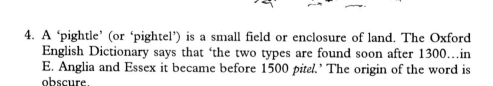

Deeks or holls?

4. A 'pightle' (or 'pightel') is a small field or enclosure of land. The Oxford English Dictionary says that 'the two types are found soon after 1300...in E. Anglia and Essex it became before 1500 *pitel.*' The origin of the word is obscure.

Author's Note: Whilst I am happy to report that another Cubitt Seiley and family still farm land at Happisburgh today, the ultimate fate of the unfortunate dickey is not known!

12. Ships That Passed in the Night

The design of the distinctive double-ender beach boat used by the east coast fishermen is usually attributed to the sleek lines of the Viking longships which first came to our shores in the ninth century, or perhaps to the earlier Saxon invaders as exemplified by the great boat burial unearthed at Sutton Hoo. However, other cultures, notably the Dutch, have also influenced the design of local craft. The following types of sailing vessels could all have been spotted off our coast in Victorian times. Can you identify their origins and purpose?

1. A snow
2. A plumper
3. A dandy
4. A billyboy
5. A yawl
6. A buss
7. A cog

The billyboy
Star of Hope

Answers

Details and illustrations of some of the vessels mentioned below may be found in *Pierhead Paintings: Ship Portraits from East Anglia* by Charles Lewis, Norfolk Museums Service (1982)

1. A 'snow' or 'snaw' comes from the Dutch *snauw* and is defined by the Oxford English Dictionary (OED) as a 'small sailing vessel resembling a brig'. Great Yarmouth Maritime Museum has a fine picture of the snow *Berbice* of London leaving Marseilles in 1828. This trading vessel was owned by Samuel Wayth of Southwold.

The snow Berbice of London

2. The word *plump* is of Dutch origin and means 'to let fall'. Before the spread of the railways, coal was transported by flat-bottomed coastal vessels from North Shields to this region. The heavily-laden ships, nicknamed 'plumpers', would wait offshore until high tide and then 'plump down' on the wide Norfolk beaches to discharge their black cargo into waiting horse-drawn carts. The next tide would refloat the lightened vessel. Cromer museum has some wonderful photographs of beached coal-ships.
'The *Ellis*, last of three coal ships to ply between the Northern coal ports and the Norfolk coast. Known locally as The Plumper, the *Ellis* was built at Hartlepool in 1858.' *Reminder of Family's Sea Links – EDP (1972)*

3. *The Daily News* of November 12th 1880 tells us that the:
'*Busy Bee*, fishing dandy, of Lowestoft, struck on a wreck and foundered'.
In the 1870s many local fishing vessels adopted the dandy-rig, a newly developed sail pattern which divided the overall sail area into several smaller sails. This gave greater flexibility, and hence better fishing prospects than the traditional lugsail rigging, but not it seems to the unfortunate crew of the *Busy Bee*. The origin of the word is unknown.

4 The OED defines 'billyboy' as a 'Humber or east coast boat' and suggests that the term is comparable with the Dutch *bijlander,* 'a vessel with one large mast sailing on the coast'. King's Lynn artist George Laidman (1872-1954) has left us a fine picture of the Billyboy *Star of Hope*, a small ketch-rigged coasting barge with leeboards which are a typical feature of Dutch vessels. Laidman served on the vessel, which was owned by his father. The picture may be seen in King's Lynn museum.

The yawl Hearts of Oak
rotting on Sea Palling beach

5 'Yawls', pronounced yolls, were the specially designed sailing and pulling beach boats used by the nineteenth century east coast Beach Companies for rescue and salvage work and were the forerunners of today's lifeboats. 'Yawl' comes from *jol,* the seventeenth century Dutch word for a small boat. We have this description by a Lowestoft resident of a launching:
'Pipes are stowed, yarns are broken, and every man makes in haste for the yawl of his own company.' *F.J. Tansley - Yachting Monthly (1898)*

6. A buss was a large (upwards of 50 gross tons) deep-sea fishing vessel which the Dutch used when catching herring off Great Yarmpouth in the seventeenth century. A roundel of Flemish glass dated 1612 in a window of No. 4 South Quay, Great Yarmouth (now a museum) gives us a wonderful picture of a high-sterned buss with its crew hauling their herring nets.

A Dutch fishing buss redrawn from the window in 4, South Quay, Great Yarmouth

7. A cog (or cogge) is a medieval vessel defined by the OED as 'a ship of burden or transport'. Great Yarmouth's St Nicholas seal, the official 'stamp of approval' of the town's powerful Admiralty Court (established by Royal Charter in 1559, abolished 1835) carries a picture of an English cog, emphasizing the importance of the port's medieval maritime trading company. Cog is Middle English from Old French *cogue*.

Great Yarmouth's St Nicholas seal

13. Smoke-screen or False Scent?

Whilst herring *(Clupea harengus)* had been landed in the ports of Great Yarmouth and Lowestoft for centuries, it was the medieval invention of the red herring, and later the kipper, which created an important food processing industry, revolutionised the east coast fishery and met the religious culinary demands of much of Roman Catholic Europe in one simple process.

The method of hanging the gutted and salted fish in a stream of smoke ensured the fish remained palatable for long enough to be boxed and transported across the North Sea to the inland regions of eastern Europe and the warmer Mediterranean countries, where a devout population insisted on eating fish every Friday to keep their faith.

Strictly, not all these words belong to the Norfolk dialect, but they are all very firmly associated with Yarmouth and Lowestoft and describe ways by which herring are preserved. Can you define the origins of the following?

1. A red herring (or Norfolk capon)
2. A kipper
3. A bloater
4. A buckling
5. Klondyking

Packing the 'silver darlings'

Answers

1 'A red herring is wholesome on a frosty morning; it is a most precious fish merchandise because it can be carried through all Europe.'
From - In Praise of Red Herring – a play by Thomas Nash (1599)
Red herrings are prepared by being first 'roused' overnight with rough salt and then smoked over smouldering oak sawdust for up to 48 hours. The smoking process, repeated two or three times over a period of two weeks, imparts a colourful browny-red hue to the fish and a distinctive flavour. This highly aromatic attribute resulted in red herrings becoming associated with laying a false scent for hounds or acting as a diversion.
'A red herring... is also known as a Norfolk capon.'
The Fishes of Gt Britain & Ireland - Francis Day (1880-1884)

2 Kipper is a Scottish word originally applied to male salmon in the breeding season when the fish would develop a bony projection, a 'kip', on their lower jaws. This beak was used by the fish as a weapon when two or more fought for the same female. When caught, these out of condition 'kipper salmon' would be split open and smoked to improve their eating qualities, and gradually the term became applied to other smoked fish including herring. The origin of *kip* is from the Low German *kippe,* a point or tip. Unlike a red herring the kipper does not need soaking prior to cooking.

3 Bloaters were 'invented' in Great Yarmouth around 1830 by a curer called Bishop. Usually bloaters are lightly salted and smoked whole with their guts intact as a more delicate, yet gamey alternative to the harsher cure of red herring. The word 'bloat' may derive from either Old Norse *blotr fiskr* meaning soft fish, or Swedish *blotfisk,* soaked fish.
'Real Yarmouth bloaters are herrings very slightly salted and smoked for three or four hours only.' *Notes and Jottings from Animal Life - Francis T. Buckland (1882)*

4 A buckling is a cure of Scottish origin where, unlike kippers and bloaters, which are cold-cured, the herring are hot-smoked, which partially cooks the fish at the same time. The OED suggests the word comes from the German *bückling* (plural *bücklinge).* Since buckling are particularly favoured by the Jewish community, perhaps the word may have Yiddish origins

5 Klondyking is the process of boxing gutted herring in a mixture of ice and salt for overseas export, a practice introduced in late Victorian times with the principal destination being the German port of Hamburg. The name comes from the 1896 Klondyke gold-rush, for indeed the advent of the steam drifter in turn-of-the-century Lowestoft brought the local fishing industry success comparable to the fortunes won in the Yukon goldfields.
'Klondykin' was started by a Low'stoft merchant old Ben Bradbeer.'
Ernie Armes quoted in Following the Fishing - David Butcher (1987)

14. The Eastern Isles

Examination of the 1:25000 Ordnance Survey sheet TG42 for Hickling Broad (Norfolk) reveals some unusual locality names in close proximity to the coast. We know from landscape studies that this stretch of coastland has changed with the rise and fall of sea levels over the centuries. When translated, the names of these unusual features can give us clues to the topography of this landscape when Dark Ages Saxon or Viking longboats nosed their way up the creeks and waterways of a Norfolk which is now much altered by the hand of man.

Can you explain the following?

    1. Delve Bank and Delph Hills (Map Ref 448257)
    2. Heigham Holmes (Map Ref 442204)
    3. Eelfleet Wall (Map Ref 451208)
    4. Old Alder Carr (Map Ref 442258)
    5. Decoy Wood (Map Ref 482209)

The Waxham decoy

Answers

1. The *Oxford English Dictionary* defines 'delph', or 'delve' as 'a hole or cavity dug in the earth for irrigation or drainage, specifically applied to the drainage canals in the fen districts of the eastern counties.' The word is from the Old English *gedelf*, whence comes the Dutch *delf*, a ditch, from which Delft, a town in Holland, takes its name.

2. Holme(s), or holm comes from the Old Norse *holmr*, 'an islet in a bay, creek, lake or river, or a meadow on the shore'. A careful examination of the map shows that all the 'holmes' in this vicinity lie on the higher ground and must have been islands in former times. They became islands once again when the great Horsey flood of February 1938 saw the sea breaching the sand dunes and flooding much of this area for many months.
The *Oxford Dictionary of English Place Names* suggests that Heigham may be Old English for high homestead, or homestead with a hedge.

3. Fleet is from an Old English word *fleth* meaning 'a place where water flows; an arm of the sea; a creek, inlet, run of water.' Eelfleet Wall is an embanked watercourse which surrounds the 'island' of Heigham Holmes. This comes from *A Perambulation of Ludham Ferthing 1338-9*:
'A traverse from Longegore [Long Gore] to Blakefleth [Blackfleet] to Iluesfleth [Eelfleet]...and from there to Martham Brodee' quoted in *The Making of the Broads (1961)*
In Norfolk, 'fleet' is also used for a train of herring nets paid out by a herring drifter.

4. The OED defines 'carr' as a fen or bog grown up with low bushes, willows, alders, etc. a boggy or fenny copse from Old Norse *kjarr*, a pool or pond. However, local usage suggests that this too may mean a small island:
'The larger islets are known as "carrs" and "alder carrs" to denote those on which the waterside tree grows thickly'. *Eastern England: From the Thames to the Humber - Walter White (1865)*

5. A decoy is a specially designed pond equipped with hoops and netting set up to lure and trap wild ducks. The word is perhaps from the Dutch *de*, meaning the, and *kool*, a cage. Given its location, this particular decoy may have a venerable significance:
'The decoy is said to have been introduced into Norfolk by Sir William Wodehouse, the Lord of Waxham Manor, in the reign of James I.' *The Battle for the Broads - Martin Ewans (1992)*

14. 'You Take the High Road'

From earliest times Norfolk's rich farmland and gentle landscape encouraged people to create settlements in this area. Continuing prosperity saw the development of a complex network of lanes and paths within and between those settlements as society developed and people traded the wares which they produced from the good land. In this way the distinctive market towns of Norfolk grew and prospered, attracting artisans and tradespeople to these centres of society. Little wonder then that we have many distinctive dialect words for these well-trodden pathways. Can you identify the origins of the following?

1. Yarmouth Rows
2. Lowestoft Scores
3. A driftway
4. A loke

Answers

1.

'Rows', found in Great Yarmouth, are very narrow medieval streets (some are barely one metre wide) which lead from the town's central market place to the quaysides. 'Row' is an Old English word meaning a single or double line of houses. It has been suggested that the Rows were deliberately kept very narrow in an effort to contain the large amounts of blown sand from which Yarmouth still suffers today. Many of the Row houses were destroyed by bombing in World War II, and subsequent re-development has obliterated much of this unique street pattern.

'...and next day the passers-by heard the Crier going up and down the Rows'. *The Rabbit Skin Cap - George Baldry (1939)*

2. Originally natural drainage channels cut (or 'scored') into the sloping river bank, 'scores' are found in Lowestoft and Beccles. Local people used them as access ways and eventually they were paved and houses built on either side. 'Score' derives from Old English *scaran*, a cut or furrow.

'There is evidence to suggest they [scores] were Neolithic tracks and all of the alleyways were originally drainage channels.' *Eastern Daily Press (August 2 1997)*

3. A 'driftway' is a local term for a drove road; 'a lane or road along which horses or cattle are driven'. One of East Anglia's greatest writers, Sir Henry Rider Haggard (1856-1925) quotes:

'The broadway that led to it...was a drift or grass lane.' *Colonel Quaritch - H. Rider Haggard (1888)*

Driftways were used more often after the eighteenth century introduction of turnpikes, mainly because the cattle didn't take to the hard surfaces and the drovers did not want to pay the tolls. *Drift* is a word of Dutch origin. The terms 'drove' or 'droveway' are more commonly used in Fenland.

4. 'In the lokes and causeys I'll seek him as my soul du love'. *The Song of Solomon in Norfolk Dialect - Rev E Gillett (1862)*

The OED defines 'loke' (or 'loak') as 'a dialect word representing the Old English *loca*, enclosed place. This is very much a Norfolk word meaning 'a lane, a short, narrow, blind lane, a cul-de-sac; a grass road, a private lane or road'.

15. Terms of Endearment

In medieval times Norfolk was the most heavily populated part of Britain with Norwich second only to London, the largest city of the kingdom. In such a society with so many people bumping into one another on a daily basis we should not be surprised that a distinctive language quickly evolved to express social interactions between neighbours. The Norfolk dialect has a number of unique expressions for greeting friends and acquaintances. Can you define the origins and meanings of the following?

1. Bor
2. Mawther (or mauther)
3. Sele of the day
4. Together

'I say, Barney bor, these bunks cut damn hard!'

Answers

1. Bor is almost certainly the shortened form of 'neighbour' for which we may find two possible derivations, both from Dutch words. *Buur,* or *buurman* is the Dutch word for neighbour, whilst *boer* is their word for farmer or homesteader, a word which was also taken by Dutch settlers to Southern Africa. In common Norfolk usage today 'bor' has largely been replaced by 'boy', a trend which perhaps stems from the fame of the Boy John or indeed the Singing Postman's famous song, 'Hev Yew Gotta Loight Boy?'
'I say Barney bor, these bunks [thistles] cut damn hard!' *quoted in Gothick Norfolk by Jennifer Westwood (1989)*
This was said by Norfolk mowers when
their scythes needed sharpening.
'Barney' was Sir Berney Brograve
(1726-circa 1800) of Waxham Hall,
who reputedly cheated the Devil in
a mowing match by 'seeding' his
opponent's portion of the crop of
black beans with iron stakes.

2. Brewer's *Dictionary of Phrase and Fable* says: 'Mawther, or morther, means a lass or wench, it is the Dutch word *'moer'*, a woman'. However the Oxford English Dictionary is less certain, suggesting the word may be a Scandinavian variant of mother, or from Old English *margeo,* meaning maiden. Both agree, however, that the word is used chiefly in East Anglia.
'A modher, or modder, mother; a girle or young wench: used all over the Eastern part of England'. *South & East Country Words - John Ray (1674)*

3. 'Sele' is defined by the OED as obsolete or dialect and means 'favourable or proper time'. The word is also used to mean 'season', thus 'hay-sele' is hay-making season, 'barley-sele' the time of sowing barley.
'As I passed ....., I gave the man the sele-of-the-day'. *The Romany Rye - George Borrow (1857)*

4. Used in addressing a group of people we have two definitions from across the county for 'together'; the first from the Vicar of Raynham who felt compelled to combine his biblical knowledge with his love of the Norfolk dialect to translate the Song of Solomon for the benefit of his parishioners!.
'Together is used as a pronoun of multitude, always in the vocative eg. "Here's a nice harvest day together" would be a salutation to a company of mowers.'
Preface to The Song of Solomon in the Norfolk Dialect - Rev E. Gillett (1862)
'It has been wittily observed, that ..together is (the) plural of bor.' *Yarmouth and Lowestoft - J. G. Nall (1866)*

16. Across the Water?

Since earliest times communication routes across Norfolk have been heavily influenced by the rivers and marshes of this low lying land. Thus bridges and causeways have always been important features of the landscape, evidenced by the ancient names which describe them. Can you define the origins of the following?

1. Acle Wey Bridge (carries the A1064 'Acle Old Road' across the River Bure)
2. Wayford Bridge (carries the A149 trunk road across the River Ant near Stalham)
3. Tonnage Bridge (carries a track across the North Walsham & Dilham Canal)
4. Carnser or Causey

The 'Caanser'

Answers

1. *Wey* is a British (i.e. pre Anglo-Saxon) river name, which appears also in the River Wey and Weybridge in Surrey. This Norfolk example may suggest that what we now call the River Bure may have been the River Wey in the tongue of the ancient Britons, with only this obscure name for the crossing point surviving to indicate its early name. The present bridge, the latest of many such structures, was completed in 1997. Another 'wey' may be found on a tributary of the Bure near St Benet's Abbey: 'The other causeway, to Ludham, leads northwards from the abbey gate and crosses the Hundred Stream where a 'small way bridge' is marked on an old map'. *St Benet's Abbey - W.F. Edwards (1983)*

2. The first element of the name Wayford could also be a corruption of the British *wey*, or of the Old English *(ge)waed* meaning a ford. But, says the Norfolk Archaeological Unit: 'more probably the etymology is the same as Wayford, Somerset, interpreted by Ekwall as the ford on the wai or made road'. *East Anglian Archaeology Report No 8. Wayford Bridge Smallburgh (1978)*
Wayford lies at the eastern end of a Roman road, The Fen Causeway, which stretches right across mid-Norfolk from Denver in the west to this crossing of the River Ant at Smallburgh. The route of the road to the east is yet to be determined.

3. 'Tonnage' is defined by the Oxford English Dictionary as 'a charge or payment per ton on cargo or freight; e.g. that payable at any port or wharf, or on a canal. Tonnage Bridge lies at the point where the River Ant becomes the North Walsham to Dilham Navigation, constructed in the 1830s to link this remoter part of North Norfolk with the rest of the Broads system. The wherrymen who plied this narrow waterway paid their dues to the canal company at this bridge according to their cargoes; corn for grinding at the mills upstream (Briggate Mill, Ebridge Mill), or bricks from the extensive Dilham brickworks. Closed in 1935, the canal is now a haven for wildlife, including the graceful otter *(Lutra lutra)*.

4. A 'carnser', 'caanser' or 'causey' is a causeway across the marshes, as these contributions from readers writing to the *Eastern Daily Press* in 1949 reveal: 'The marsh road, linking Cantley ferry with the village of Langley is known as the Caanser'. *Broad Norfolk - T.H.Cooper (EDP January 21st-March 19th 1949)*
'Our village is divided by the mill dam, a causeway. During last week's gale we were told: 'Do you mind how you go over the mill caanser, do you'll get hut [hurt].' *Broad Norfolk - D.M.S (EDP January 21st-March 19th 1949)* `

17. Creepier Crawlies?

In an agricultural county like Norfolk the accumulated wisdom of all things to do with the land is close to the heart of every countryman. So we should not be surprised that the Norfolk dialect is peppered with all sorts of special names for the creatures which inhabit the countryside. This collection of Norfolk names comprises some of the smaller, many-legged creatures of our fields and hedgerows, all that is except the last, which is the Norfolk name applied to two birds that, given the opportunity, include the others in their diet! Can you sort out who is eating what?

1. Bishee-barny bee
2. Pishmire or pissamare
3. Cleg
4. Erriwiggle
5. King-Harry

*King-Harry or
Goldfinch*

Answers

1. A 'Bishee-Barny Bee' is a Norfolk ladybird *(Coccinella sp)*, perhaps named after Bishop Barnabas.
   'Bishee-Barny Bee, the little spotted beetle commonly called the Lady-cow or Lady-bird.' *South and East Country Words - John Ray (1674)*
   Saint Barnabas (1st century AD) was the preaching companion of Saint Paul and may have been the first Bishop of Milan. The red coat of the ladybird perhaps reflects the colour of the bishop's vestments, and of course the insects flourish on Barnabas' feast-day, June 11th.

2. A 'pishmire' or 'pissamare' is a dialect word (now obsolete) for an ant *(Formicidae sp)*, derived, says the OED, 'from piss + mire from the urinous smell of the ant'. The word comes from the Dutch *pismiere*.
   'Blowed if that wornt an oul pishamare, he'd bin a setting on a pishamares' nearst.' *The Boy John Letters - Sidney Grapes (June 28th 1950)*

3. A 'cleg' is a Norfolk horsefly *(Tabanus sudeticus)* or gadfly. The name comes from the Old Norse *Kleggi*.
   'For animals of their size "clegs" are exceedingly light -footed.' *Daily News August 24 1872*

4. An 'erriwiggle' is an earwig *(Forficula auricularia)*.
   'If it be determined, after Dr Wallis and some other entomologist, that earwig comes from *eruca*, in the like manner as periwig from perruque, our word is certainly a great improvement on that formation.' *The Vocabulary of East Anglia - Robert Forby (1830)*
   Eruca (or *eruque*) is the Latin for caterpillar. Alternatively, Jonathan Mardle in *Broad Norfolk* also quotes 'pishamare-barneybee' as a Norfolkism for an earwig.

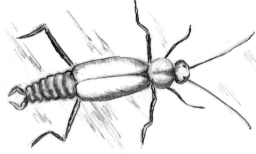

5. 'King-Harry is a popular name of two common singing birds.
   1. King Harry Redcap is the gold-finch, *Fringilla carduelis*
   2. King Harry Blackcap, is the bird which is commonly called simply the Blackcap, *Motacilla atricapilla*.
   The Vocabulary of East Anglia - Robert Forby (1830)

18. Taking the Waters

The following are all names of tributaries of Norfolk rivers, mostly the River Wensum as it flows through Norwich. Not surprisingly many of these obscure tributaries have Scandinavian names for in the year 1004 the Danish King Swein Forkbeard (died 1014) sacked Norwich and took control of much of East Anglia. In his book entitled *Norwich* (English Heritage 1994) Brian Ayers, describes these long-forgotten streams and defines the evidence which reveals their existence. By painstaking research he has shown how their location had a fundamental effect upon the pattern of early settlement in the Anglo-Scandinavian town which has now become the City of Norwich. Can you say where they occur, and how they got their names?

1. Great Cockey
2. Muspole
3. Dallingfleet
4. Dalymond
5. Scarrow Beck

Answers

1. A number of small tributary streams flow through central Norwich, which are known locally as 'cockeys'. The largest of these, Great Cockey, rises in All Saints Green, flows under the Back of the Inns and Little London Street. London Street itself was formerly Cockey Street. Great Cockey finally joins the Wensum near St George's Bridge, where the mouth of the culvert which contains it can still be seen. The word 'cockey' derives from the Saxon for water and the Celtic word for hollow.

2. The Muspole is another Norwich cockey. Rising near St Mary's Plain its course is still delineated by Muspole Street, from where it flows beneath Colegate, joining the Wensum near Fye Bridge. We can be fairly sure that the second element of the name is a corruption of 'pool', whilst the OED gives 'muss' as a dialect word for mouth from the Old French *muse*.

3. The Dallingfleet cockey rises near the site of the Franciscan friary (at the top of Prince of Wales Road) and flows eastwards via the sinuous St Faith's Lane to join the main river south of the Cathedral Close at Rushworth's Staithe. Fleet is from *fleth*, an Old English word meaning 'a place where water flows'. (See p. 37) 'Dalling' may also be from the Old English *dael*, meaning a small valley. 'Names in *dal-* and *-dale* are most frequent in the Old Scandinavian districts and mostly contain Old Norse

dalr, Old Swedish *dal*, a valley'. Concise Oxford Dictionary of English Place Names.

4. We may be seeing this same *dale* element in the name of the Dalymond cockey, which flows from north of the city at Old Catton, follows the line of Edward and Peacock Streets and joins the main river at Hansard (formerly Water) Lane.

8. Beck is well known as a north country word for a small stream or brook. However, it is also found in Norfolk; Scarrow Beck rises near East Beckham and joins the Bure near Blickling. The word comes from the Old Norse *bekkr* and was almost certainly introduced into Norfolk and elsewhere by the Viking invaders. Scarrow may be from Old Norse *skaro*, a gap or notch, i.e. a valley.

Norwich cockeys

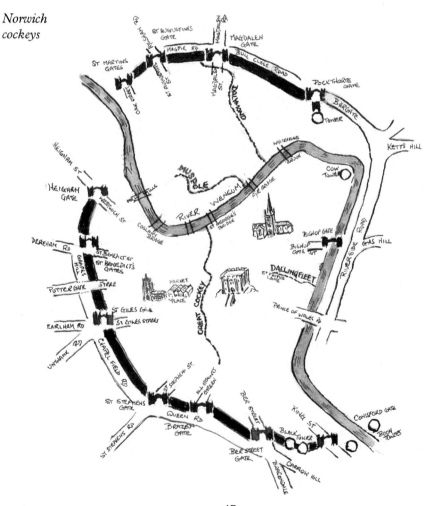

47

19. Spinning a Good Yarn

In medieval times Norfolk was one of the most prosperous parts of the country, with Norwich the second city of the land after London. It was the cloth trade upon which this prosperity was firmly based. The industry was flourishing by the late twelfth century and was further enhanced in the fourteenth century by the influx of Flemish weavers. More of their countrymen, 'The Strangers', came over in the sixteenth and seventeenth centuries and exerted much influence on the development of Norwich. In the nineteenth century the Industrial Revolution caused the weaving industry to move northwards to Yorkshire and Lancashire, forcing the Norwich industry to specialise in fine quality silk shawl and *crepe de chine* production. The last remnant of this great industry only disappeared from Norfolk in the early 1990s with the closure of Grout's Mill in Great Yarmouth, which for many years had specialised in producing woven crepe bandages. These words and place names are all connected with the medieval cloth industry, can you identify the origin and meaning of the following?

1 Worstead (8 miles north-east of Aylsham)
2 Hempstead (3 miles south-east of Holt)
3 Lucum (or loucum)
4 Litester

Grout's weaving mill, Great Yarmouth

Answers

1. Renowned for its hard-wearing qualities the name and reputation of worsted cloth quickly spread throughout medieval Europe and the resultant wealth from this export trade helped to build many of our magnificent East Anglian churches. Production of woollens and worsteds was concentrated around Norwich and also in villages to the north-east of the city in the vicinity of North Walsham. Thus it is fitting that the fourteenth century church in the village of Worstead, from where the cloth got its name, remains a particularly fine example of ecclesiastical architecture described by the English writer, Arthur Mee, as 'like a small cathedral'. *The King's England, Norfolk - Arthur Mee (1940)* Worstead is Old English and means 'site of the enclosure'.

2. The weaving of coarse linen in Norfolk was also important in medieval times, but it differed from the wool trade in that most of the linen was sold locally for domestic and agricultural purposes rather than being exported. Whereas fine linen was made from flax, the raw material for this linen was hemp *(Cannabis sativa)*, and Hempstead is simply 'the place where hemp (in Old English *henep)* was grown.'

3. Whilst the cottage-based worsted industry was firmly established in early Norman times, by the late fourteenth century a need for more skilled workers was resolved by Edward III (1312-1377) and his Queen Phillipa, who were instrumental in encouraging Flemish weavers to settle in Norfolk. A *lucum* is the word these Flemish workers used to describe the distinctive large dormer windows by which they illuminated their cottage workshops to assist them in their labours. You can still find 'lucums' in cottages in the North Walsham area today. The word is related to the present day Dutch word *luiken,* meaning a dormer window.

4. The production of worsted was a labour-intensive enterprise with individuals or small groups of weavers working the looms and the spinning undertaken by the women and children of the family. A 'litester' is a medieval term for a dyer, from lye, a strong alkali used in the washing of wool. A famous litester of Felmingham, John Litester, challenged the authority of the crown when Richard II introduced a poll tax in 1381.

Geoffrey the dyer's 16th century house in Worstead

49

20. Longshore Warriors

All the following terms describe the ways by which the nineteenth century beachmen of Great Yarmouth and Gorleston sought to earn what often proved to be a precarious living from the sea. Living and working on the shore as co-operative Beach Companies these brave and tough seafarers had to be opportunistic in the extreme in order to survive, their principal source of income being the salvage monies resulting from the many sailing vessels which foundered on the deadly east coast sandbanks. Through all this however these 'longshore warriors' (or 'longshore sharks' as some claimed) rarely faltered in defining their priorities between saving vessels and saving lives, for they established the principles upon which today's much-respected Royal National Lifeboat Institution (RNLI) was founded. Can you define the following rather curious terms describing the ways in which they made their diverse livings?

1. Hovelling
2. Overing
3. Swiping
4. Swinging
5. Free trade
6. Pleasuring

Towing out the bathing machines

Answers

As defined in *The Beachmen* by David Higgins (1987)

1. 'Hovel' was the beachmen's general term for salvage money derived from saving vessels or retrieving flotsam, (floating objects) jetsam, (objects cast or 'jettisoned' on to the shore) or 'lagan' (material lying on the seabed). The OED defines 'hoveller' as: 'An unlicensed pilot or boatman, frequently applied to a boatman who goes out to wrecks, sometimes with a view of plunder' . A 'hovel' is also the name for the boat used for this purpose; the origin of the word is obscure.

2. 'Overing' was the special word used for ferrying passengers across the River Yare from Gorleston to South Denes. Overing was especially lucrative on race days when the old Yarmouth race-course was located on the Denes. However, following the closure of the Birds Eye factory in the 1980s and the disappearance of the commuters who worked there, the ferry service struggled to survive on a commercial basis and closed in 1998.

3. 'Swiping' was the term used for retrieving anchors, lost in the inevitable mishaps which occurred when sailing vessels were compelled to heave-to in Yarmouth roads, often for weeks on end, awaiting favourable winds. Payment for any anchors retrieved varied according to whether the anchor's location had been marked by a buoy, with a higher fee being applied to searching for and securing unmarked losses.

4. Brush Bend, the essential ninety-degree turn of the River Yare engineered in late medieval times to ensure the stability of the harbour's mouth, has always proved a test to navigation, especially to sailing vessels in difficult wind conditions. Many of the beachmen, although unlicensed, were skilled pilots in their own right, well experienced in using small boats to run out lines to the mooring dolphins to 'swing' large vessels around the bend and bring them safely to berth at the quayside.

5. 'Free-trade' was the euphemism used all along the east coast for smuggling, an activity which, given the precarious nature of a beachman's existence, provided a temptation to which some inevitably succumbed.

6. The growth of Yarmouth and Gorleston in the nineteenth century as popular holiday resorts offered lucrative opportunities to the beachmen to provide pleasure trips from the beach for the visitors during the summer months. In the early days 'pleasuring' also included the provision of bathing machines; today's deck-chair and beach-hut operators are a surviving branch of this general trade.

51

21. Naming the Parts

The Cromer crab fishery has flourished on a fully commercial basis since mid-Victorian times and the catching and processing of these tasty shellfish remains an important north Norfolk enterprise. The methods employed to catch only mature crabs by baited pots (immature crabs are returned live to the sea) are more akin to farming and husbandry, practices which hopefully will ensure the long term sustainability of the fishery. All the following words refer to parts or forms of the edible crab *(Cancer pagurus)*, can you say to what they refer and why they are used in this way?

1. Cart
2. Shekel
3. Deaf ears
4. Toggs
5. Whitetoes (or whitefeet)

The edible crab

Answers

1. When selling a crab a good fishmonger will detach the main shell of the crustacean from the rest of the body to demonstrate to the customer that the brown meat inside is plentiful, firm and wholesome. This detached shell in some parts of Norfolk is called the 'cart', but the term 'boat' is also used. The word 'cart' is closely related to the word 'crate'; both may derive from the German *kratte* meaning a basket or pannier.

2. The word 'shekel' refers to the internal shell of the crab which contains the vital organs and supports the legs of the creature. Shekel is a dialect pronunciation of *shackle*, a word of German and Dutch origin with a number of meanings, including the links of a chain or fetter. It only takes a slight stretch of the imagination to associate the complex arched structure of the crab's shekel with these chains once used for hobbling animals.

3. 'Deaf ears' is a local Norfolk term for the feathery grey gills of the animal, structures which the rest of the world calls 'dead-men's fingers'. Although quite edible in themselves, deaf ears are usually discarded to avoid eating any harmful micro-organisms which they may have entrapped.

4. 'Toggs' is a traditional term for immature crabs which don't meet the legal size (115mm across the broadest part of the cart); when caught, these under-sized crabs must by law be immediately returned to the sea. Legislation to control the fishery was first introduced into Norfolk in the 1870s following an investigation by Francis Buckland (1826-1880) acting on behalf of the government. His *Report on the Fisheries of Norfolk* states:
'The cause of the decrease of the crab and lobster fisheries is first, the wholesale destruction of small crabs called "Toggs" or "Short Crabs", and second, destruction of crabs and lobsters in spawn.'
Togg may be a dialect corruption of *teg* or *tegg*, a term of Scandinavian origin defined by the OED as 'a sheep or deer in its second year.'

5. White-toes are recently moulted crabs with distinctive white tips to their usually black main claws, which indicate that they are about to spawn. Although of legal size, by law they must not be landed. This regulation is part of the effort to conserve the fishery. The crabbing season has usually begun by early March when the creatures come out of 'hibernation'. In a typical year the catches drop around mid-July, and pick up again through September. Inclement weather and hibernation will usually bring the season to a close by late October.
'Between the 1st day of November and the 30th day of June following (both days inclusive) no person shall remove from a fishery any edible crab *(Cancer pagurus)* of the kind known as whitefooted crab'. *Eastern Sea Fisheries Joint Committee By-law No 10*

22. A Man is as Good as His Word!

The following words, phrases and places are (mostly) a familiar part of our language today but it was not always so. They have all come to enrich the English language by the renown of one of Norfolk's sons, and as such must surely claim to be pure Norfolk dialect? Can you identify the men who gave us these words, what they mean and why they have lingered in our language?

1. Hansard
2. Manby's Apparatus
3. Vancouver Island
4. ...and just how did Brewer enrich our language?

Captain Manby's Apparatus

Answers

1 Hansard is the name given to the written record of Parliamentary Sessions. Luke Hansard (1752-1828), a Norwich-born printer, left the parish of Coslany at the age of 18 to seek his fortune in London. He did well, eventually owning the company which was contracted to print the *House of Commons Journal*, an unofficial account of proceedings written by William Cobbett (1762-1835) of *Rural Rides* fame. Luke's firm of Hansard remained independent until 1889 when it was taken over by the Stationery Office. Coincidentally, Her Majesty's Stationery Office relocated in the 1960s to a building in Norwich that lies a very close to Luke Hansard's birthplace. Hansard Lane (formerly Water Lane) is named in his honour.

2. The phrase 'Manby's Apparatus' comes from Norfolk-born Captain George Manby (1765-1854), Barrack Master at Great Yarmouth, whose invention of a mortar line-throwing apparatus for saving lives at sea has secured his name a place in our language. When on February 12th, 1808, the brig *Elizabeth* of Plymouth foundered on a sandbank just off Great Yarmouth, Manby successfully fired off his mortar line and the sailors aboard secured it to the vessel. Manby despatched a small ballasted row-boat to the *Elizabeth* and when it returned to the shore was rewarded by seeing seven sodden survivors crawl up the beach. It was a triumph, and all along the coast life-saving companies were soon formed, saving an estimated 1,000 lives. With minor modifications to a rocket-firing method, Manby's 'gun' or 'apparatus' was in use until the end of the last century.

3. The great explorer George Vancouver (1757-1798) gave his name, and the names of other notable Norfolk residents, to the area surrounding Vancouver Island on the north-west coast of Canada. So we find a Port Coke (after Thomas Coke (1754-1842) of Holkham) and Port Windham (after the Norfolk statesman William Windham) rubbing shoulders with Lynn Channel, Port Snettisham and Holkham Bay, all of which reminded the great man of his Norfolk origins, for he was born in King's Lynn. Sadly, however, one name which Vancouver conferred has not survived: 'With three volleys of musketry, Alaska was claimed for King George, under the name of New Norfolk'. *The East Wind by Jane Hales (1969)*

4. Anyone who is interested in words will soon become familiar with Brewer's *Dictionary of Phrase and Fable*, but may not know that it was compiled by master wordsmith Reverend Ebenezer Cobham Brewer LL.D (1810-1897). Brewer's father was headmaster of Mile End House Boarding School, and young Brewer taught there before moving on to greater things. Brewer's famous dictionary contains many references to Norfolk dialect, but his greatest triumph must be that it has firmly stood the test of time:
'The Derivation, Source, or Origin of Common Places, Allusions and Words that have a Tale to Tell.'

23. Meet the Flintstones!

All the following words are connected with flint (Silicon Dioxide, SiO_2), a hard glassy substance occurring naturally within beds of chalk (Calcium Carbonate $CaCO_3$), upon which the very fabric of Norfolk is founded; indeed generations upon generations of East Anglians have used both flint and chalk as cutting tools, weapons and building materials since time immemorial. Neolithic man mined the chalk of Breckland at Grimes Graves to exploit the best quality flint found some thirty feet (10m.) below the surface. From this material were made the remarkable tools which were used by succeeding generations to fashion the landscape, whilst the flint cobbles of our fields and beaches have provided the material for the distinctive and magnificent architecture which is so special to Norfolk.

Flint comes in a variety of distinctive forms. Can you define the following peculiar varieties of flint?

1. Hag-stones
2. Belemnites
3. Paramoudra (or potstones)
4. Floorstone
5. Sarsens (or sarses)
6. ....and why are they called Grimes Graves?

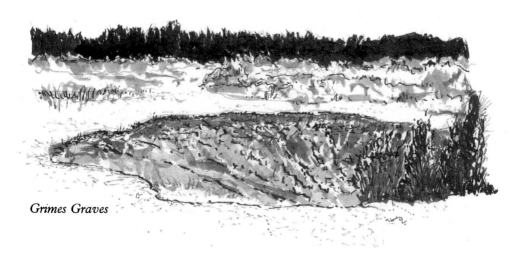

Grimes Graves

Answers

1. 'Hag-stones' are those flint nodules which contain a hole through the middle; such curiosities are considered to be of magical origin, esteemed by some as lucky tokens. The word hag, derived from Old English *haegtesse*, means a witch. A distinguishing features of such beings, it was claimed, was a completely circular mouth; hence the link with a round hole in a stone. The word is also applied to the parasitic hag-fish *(Myxine glutinosa)* which has a circular sucker by which it attaches itself to its host. Many believe that the hole in a hag-stone is produced by the erosive action of dripping water; however, geologists suggest that the hole is formed when a fossil, often a belemnite, falls out of the surrounding flint nodule in which it was encased.

2. Belemnites are the bullet-shaped remains of ancient sea creatures which resembled modern squids. Geologists believe that the distinctive shape represents a flint-filled cavity of the creature's body, the rest of which is rarely preserved. Belemnites may be found in situ within the chalk deposits formed in the Cretaceous seas which covered Norfolk some 120 million years ago, and of course you can search for them in the shingle of the wide beaches of Norfolk where they lie after erosion from the nearby cliffs. Known locally as 'devil's thunderbolts' or 'thunderstones' they supposedly fell during thunderstorms. The word is from the Greek *belemnon*, a dart.

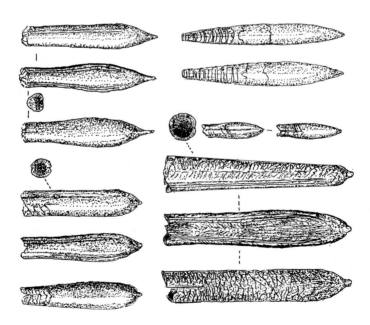

3. 'Paramoudra', or pot-stones, also have a hole through the middle, but these are large pear-shaped lumps of flint (up to one metre in diameter) which may often be found stacked one on top of another forming four-five metre vertical pipes within the chalk strata. Their existence is attributed to enormous worms that lived in vertical burrows in the seabed of the Cretaceous sea. Whilst not unique to Norfolk (they are also found in Antrim, N. Ireland), paramoudra can often be found gracing Norfolk gateways. The Geological Society of Norfolk was founded as The Paramoudra Club by pupils of the City of Norwich Grammar School in 1950. The name probably derives from the Gaelic *peira muireach* meaning 'sea pears'.

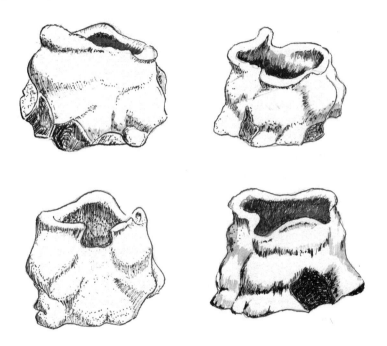

4. The Neolithic miners (*circa* 2500yrs BC) of Grimes Graves knew a thing or two about the properties of flint, especially the way in which it breaks to form a razor sharp edge when struck with a bone hammer or flaked with a hardened wooden awl. Flints found at the surface proved to be too dry and brittle, and hence unpredictable in the way they split when worked, so the miners went to considerable effort to mine the virgin flint which occurs in horizontal discontinuous bands within the chalk strata some ten metres below the surface. Eighteenth and nineteenth century workers producing gun flints for muskets found similar problems, and both groups exploited these black tabular blocks of flint which came to be known as *floorstone*.

5. In Norfolk the general name for seams of flint (floorstone, wallstone etc.) is 'sarsens', a word often applied to the massive standing stones of Stonehenge. Chambers' dictionary suggests that the word may be related to Saracen, however the link is certainly obscure.

'Seams of flint (are) referred to as "sarses" or "sarsens."' *Craft Vocabularies by A. J. Forrest in the Eastern Daily Press March 11 1949*

6. The name Grime's Graves 'was probably given to the site by the Anglo-Saxons...they thought that the mines were connected with Woden, their chief god, when they attached to them the name Grim...(the name is also found in the Hundred of Grimshoe in which Grime's Graves lie) ....'the suffix "graves" merely means hollows or workings'.

Grime's Graves Norfolk - R Rainbird Clarke HMSO (1963)
Grimr (the masked one) is another name for Woden.

Paramoudra at the gate.

24. Covering the Thatcher's Art

Norfolk would not be Norfolk without its distinctive reed-thatched buildings; indeed they stand as an icon of the county exemplifying its rural and agrarian culture. Obtained from the indigenous wetlands, Common Reed *(Phragmites communis)* grows naturally in Broadland, but in order to produce a sound product reed beds need careful management by the application of ancient skills. And so it is with the art of the thatcher. Fashioning the natural material to provide a weather-proof covering relies on skills and techniques which have come down to us from our ancestors.

Thus we should not be surprised that the thatcher's language is as old as his craft. Can you identify the meaning of the following ancient terms?

1. Yelms
2. Gavels
3. Toadying
4. Brotches

Answers

1. A 'yelm' (or 'yellum') is a bundle of conveniently-sized reed or straw prepared to enable the thatcher to tuck it under his arm for laying on the roof. The word is also used as a verb describing this action. Forby gives as derivation the Anglo-Saxon *haelm*, heap, or *gelm* or *gylm*, a bundle.
'I...started to pull the straw at the bottom of the heap and got enough to make one yellum.' *The Rabbit Skin Cap - George Baldry (1939)*

2. Similarly, the term 'gavel' is used generally to describe heaps of mown corn ready to be tied, but as the following quote shows the word is also specifically used by the thatcher as a noun and a verb:
'Not every thatcher's assistant turns out to be a good 'gaveller'. The art of it lies in making each gavel (thatch bundle) just wide enough to fit the thatcher's reach...' *Craft Vocabularies - A.J.Forrest (1949)*
Chambers Dictionary quotes gavel as a dialect form of gable. The OED identifies the word as coming from the Old Norman French *gavelle* (fem), *gavel* (masc.) meaning a heap.

3. Every thatcher had his 'toad', usually a young lad who would do all the fetching and carrying for the thatcher who was up the ladder putting on the roof.
'Toadying meant wetting the straw, shaking it evenly into a bed, then pulling it into gavels or yelms which Master Toad thereafter placed slantwise in his yoke - a fork-shaped holder - and, hoisting the yoke on his shoulders, bore his burden to the man on the roof.'
Craft Vocabularies - A.J.Forrest (1949)

4. 'Brotches' (or 'broaches') are rods of willow *(Salix alba)* or hazel *(Corylus avellana)* which the thatcher twists into a shape resembling a long legged staple. With their sharpened ends brotches are used to pierce and pin down the reed to fix the bundles permanently to the roof. As with many apparently simple devices, brotches rely on the skill of the thatcher to enable the device to grip the reed efficiently. He must impart a particular twist to the wood which will give the brotch sufficient springiness without actually breaking the rod in two. In later years brotches have been made from iron or steel. The word is from the French *broche*, a skewer.

Sharpened and twisted hazel spar

'To prevent the wind from blowing it off he pegs it down slightly with double broaches.' *The Rural Economy of Norfolk - William Marshall (1787)*

61

25. Beggar Thy Neighbour

All of the following are Norfolk words connected with some form of begging or 'scrounging', an activity which any proud Norfolk dumpling would not wish to admit to in a hurry! However, in a modern society which enjoys the safety net of a Welfare State it is all too easy for us to forget that in times past the world, especially rural Norfolk, could be a harsh and cruel place where 'survival of the fittest' had a very real meaning. The poor were forced by circumstance to live on their wits and try to get by as best they could. Can you say just how the following activities helped them, often quite honourably, in 'getting by'?

1. Mumping
2. Pawkin(g) (or porkin)
3. Largesse
4. Kittywitching
5. ...and just who was Billy Bluelight?

'They still go pawkin on Sea Palling beach'

Answers

1. 'Mumping' is the Norfolk word for begging. Rev. Forby (1830) says that a mumper is a beggar, and specifically refers to 'those who only go in troops from house to house, in some places on St Thomas' day (29 December), in others on St Stephen's (Boxing Day, 26 December). Forby suggests that the word comes form the Danish *mompelen*, to mutter or mumble or cheat. 'Has anyone remembered that elderly widows went "mumping" on Maundy Thursday?' *Broad Norfolk - S.K. (1949)*

2. 'Pawkin', or 'porkin' is what the rest of the world knows as beachcombing; the word is also known inland as 'the act of gathering firewood'.
'They still go pawkin on Sea Palling beach.' *Broad Norfolk - Swede Norah (1949)*
'Pawk' is given in the OED as dialect for 'trick, artifice, cunning device'.

3. Largesse is a country word meaning 'a gift to reapers in harvest'. Traditionally Norfolk farm workers would solicit this gift at the end of harvest by crying out 'hallo largesse', a phrase which Forby suggests is a corruption of the Norman-French *à la largesse*, which we learn was applied to 'the gifts of the onlookers to the winners in the tourneys.'
Broad Norfolk - A.J. Rudd (1949)

4. Forby gives several definitions for a *kitch-witch*, including 'a woman dressed in grotesque and frightful manner'. 'It was customary', he says 'at Yarmouth, for women of the lowest order to go in troops from house to house to levy contributions, at some season of the year', dressed in men's shirts with blood-smeared faces. 'These hideous beldams have long discontinued their perambulations but in memory of them one of the many rows in that town is called Kitty-witch row.'

5. Billy Bluelight was the nickname of William Cullum (1859-1949), a much-loved Norwich street character who would supplement his meagre income selling matches and cough medicine by loping along the riverbank near Foundry Bridge and challenging the *Jenny Lind* steamboat to a race. Billy's verbal dexterity in proposing this apparently unequal venture would usually elicit a few coppers from the amused passengers. One of Billy's favourite sayings was:

    'My name is Billy Bluelight, my age is 45
    I hope to get to Carrow Bridge before the boat arrive!'
    R. L. Potter in a letter to the EDP July 1954

As you can see the rhyme only works in the Norfolk dialect.
Billy's ability as a natural athlete rarely let him down, and as the boat steamed into Carrow, Whitlingham, Coldham Hall or even Yarmouth there would be Billy, resplendent in running shorts, sports cap and medals, waiting to greet the boat to collect his tips.

26. Games People Play

The following are all related to games, pastimes and entertainments in which the people of Norfolk somewhat peculiarly indulged themselves in times past, and also more recently. But beware! Number one is certainly not all that it seems, and numbers three and four have not, as yet, taken a permanent place in Norfolk's rich dialect heritage, but they are working on it! Can you say what on earth is going on here?

1. Camping
2. Tittermatortering or titter-cum-tortering
3. Dwile flonking
4. ...and just what is a Yarmouth Yank?

Tittermatortering

Answers

1. Camping, (or camp-ball) was an early, and more violent form of football popular in the eighteenth century. The games were usually held between village teams of a dozen or so players where the object was to get the ball between the other's goalposts by any means possible. Fisticuffs, wrestling, hacking and gouging all played their part in this exercise.

'I have heard old persons speak of a celebrated camping, Norfolk against Suffolk, on Diss common with 300 on each side....the Suffolk men, after 14 hours were the victors. Nine deaths were the result of the contest, within a fortnight.' *Spurden's supplement to Robert Forby's Vocabulary of East Anglia (1858)*

Camping-land was the place where the sport took place; there was a Camping Field abutting the churchyard at Swaffham and others at East Bilney and Stiffkey. You will still find a Campingfield Lane in Stalham today. The OED derives camp from the French *champ* a field.

2. The OED defines 'teeter' as a dialect word meaning 'to see-saw', thus in Norfolk a 'tittermatorter' ('teetermatorter' or 'titter-cum-torter') is a child's see-saw. The author recalls that there were two different see-saws in Norwich's Heigham Park playground in the 1950s, but only one was referred to by us children as a teetermatorter. This had a motion which is emulated today, by the ride known as 'The Pirate Boat'; it is just as well that the Heigham Park teetermatorter, has now been removed, for I can vouch that it contributed to more than one broken limb.

3. I seem to remember that dwile flonking made its first appearance around the time that Allan Smethurst (1927-2000), 'The Singing Postman', (see p. 41) took the nation by storm and introduced the world to the delights of dialect Norfolk with his hit record 'Hev Yew Got a Loight, Boy?'.

'Dwile flonking is a spoof game introduced in the 1960s and first played in the Bungay area.' *The Mardler's Companion - Robert Malster (1999)*

A dwile is a Norfolk floorcloth (from the Dutch *dweil,* a clout or swab: Brewer's *Dictionary of Phrase & Fable*) and is perhaps one of the better known Norfolk dialect words, but 'flonking' has no discernible pedigree, unless someone out there knows better!

The game is played by one person, holding a chamber pot containing a dwile soaked in beer, standing in the middle of a ring of players who, whilst holding hands, dance round in a circle. The dwile is then flung, or 'flonked' at one of the dancers, with the intention of hitting them whilst their attention is diverted. Since the game also calls for a heavy consumption of beer the players are indeed often diverted! Whether or not anyone has ever bothered to keep a score, or complete a dwile flonk and stay sober, is open to question. Given the current state of farming both they, and dwile flonking, could shamefully be heading for oblivion.

Dwile flonking?

4. The influx of the oil companies to Great Yarmouth in the 1960s brought a wide range of specialist workers to the town, often from the US states of Texas or Louisiana. They worked on the offshore drilling rigs, usually on a two-week-on, one-week-off basis. With exotic working titles such as driller, tool pusher, roustabout or roughneck these men invariably proved to be larger than life characters with quixotic lifestyles, generous natures and ample pay packets to match. In their week off they were keen to pursue all the things which were denied them when on the rig, i.e. a stiff drink, live country music and some female company. The entertainment gurus of Great Yarmouth were just the people to provide the first two in good measure, and not surprisingly the third was quick to follow! Many local people were drawn to such a free-wheeling carefree lifestyle. Thus it was not long before local entertainers and others were to be seen around town sporting an authentic cowboy outfit, complete with snakeskin boots, ten gallon hat and affected southern drawl. Yarmouth Yanks had been born!

Bob Orrell, a radio operator on the ill fated *Hewett A Platform,* which suffered a disastrous blow-out in November 1968, describes them thus: 'They adopted the oilman's dress, his speech and mannerisms, chewed gum or smoked large cigars and were so ludicrous they were dubbed Yarmouth Yanks by the British rigmen'. *Blow-Out by Robert Orrell (1989)*

The Yarmouth Yank

27. Do Different!

'Do different' is a phrase often quoted as the Norfolk motto, suggesting that a sense of uniqueness in all things is something to be cherished by the inhabitants of this distinctive region of the British Isles. Little wonder then that the University of East Anglia has also chosen 'Do Different' as its motto. All the following words look and, even in the Norfolk accent, sound reasonably familiar to anyone who speaks English. But in Norfolk their meaning is quite different. Indeed, it is the distinctive use of familiar words in an entirely different sense or grammatical construction which distinguishes a true dialect from merely a different accent of the same language. Can you say what these words mean in the Norfolk dialect, and explain how they may be used to 'do different'?

1. Do
2. Don't
3. Funny
4. Gather
5. Gays

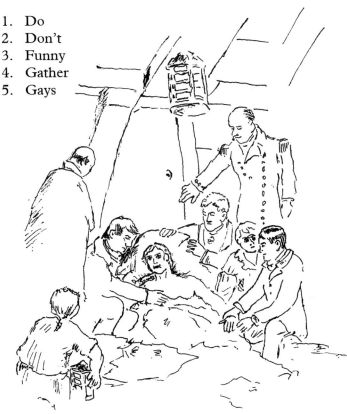

'Do you anchor, Hardy!'

Answers

1. The use of the word 'do' distinguishes a Norfolk speaker like no other, for whilst it is only a small word, in Norfolk it is used to convey a wealth of meanings. 'Do' may be used as a conjunction (which joins sentences or phrases), an adverb (which modifies a verb or adjective), an interjection ('thrown in' to express emotions) or as an imperative (expressive of command, advice or request). As such 'do' is synonymous with a number of words or phrases such as 'if', 'or', 'even if', 'yet', 'if so', 'but', or 'otherwise'; though the words 'though' or 'even though' come closest to the true meaning. 'Though' comes from Old English *theah*, but the modern German word for though, *doch*, gives us a clue to the true origin of 'do'. Two examples, the first containing the usual form and the Norfolk do:
'He told me not to do it do (i.e. otherwise) I should get wrong.'
Broad Norfolk - Anthony Hamond, Norwich (1949)
Robert Malster gives us the following example of an imperative 'do' from the lips of Admiral Lord Nelson (1758-1805) as he lay dying aboard the *Victory* at the close of the Battle of Trafalgar: 'Do you anchor, Hardy!'
Quoted in The Mardler's Companion - Robert Malster (1999)

2. In a complementary vein the Norfolk speaker's use of the negative means that the word 'don't' becomes 'if not', as in this example:
'Shet yin gate, Tim bor, don't them pigs'll git out!' *The Song of Solomon in Norfolk Dialect - Rev. E Gillett (1862)*

3. Funny is used colloquially in Norfolk as an emphatic; typical synonyms include 'extremely' or 'greatly'. 'For instance people say that something is 'funny good' *Broad Norfolk - Ian Rowarth (1949)*
The derivation of this usage is obscure, and since it is not mentioned by nineteenth century dialecticians it would seem to have come into general use at some time in the late Victorian period.

4. Gather in Norfolk means 'to become inflamed'. The OED gives many definitions including : 'to gather head', which it says, 'can mean to acquire strength; also to swell as a festering sore.'
'The Time will come that foule Sinne, gathering head, shall breake into corruption.' *Chronicle of the Kings of England - Sir Richard Baker (1643)*

5. The word 'gay' is often cited as an example of how words in the English language can evolve different meanings over time, with some expressing concern over its modern usage in referring to sexual preferences, rather than its earlier more innocent meaning of being pleasantly happy. In Norfolk, however, when someone talks of 'the gays' they are simply referring to the pictures or illustrations in a popular book or periodical.
'...Granfar hed bin a readen yar *Evenen News* ...with sum good pictures in. Granfar call 'em gays.' *Sidney Grapes – The Boy John Letters, June 23rd 1951*

28. Food for Thought

Given the agricultural heart of Norfolk, an emphasis on good food and fine cuisine is to be expected, and the residents of these parts can claim to equal the culinary passion of our Continental neighbours. So when some of those neighbours made prolonged visits to our eastern shores, their eating habits and special foods were quickly assimilated by the natives and claimed as their own. All the following words describe foodstuffs which are, or were, unique to Norfolk. Can you say what they are, and how they acquired their distinctive names?

1. Biffins
2. Coquilles
3. Floaters (or swimmers)
4. Sinkers
5. Norfolk asparagus
6. Hollow biscuits

Biffins

Coquilles

Answers

1. Biffins are sugar-coated apples, traditionally prepared by Norwich bakers; the fruit is lightly pressed between layers of straw and slowly baked for several hours in a cool oven. This slow baking intensifies the sweetness of the fruit, making them especially attractive as a treat for youngsters. The name Biffin comes from the Beaufin apples traditionally used for this confection, a variety of apple originally grown in Normandy.
'The original Beaufin (or Biffin) apple still exists in a few gardens, but a Blenheim apple gives good results.' *Mary Norwak – A Taste of Norfolk*

2. Coquilles are spiced cakes traditionally eaten in Norfolk on Shrove Tuesday or Ash Wednesday as a prelude to Lent. The small sweetmeats would often be baked in cockle shells to take on their distinctive shape, imitating the badge often worn by pilgrims who had been to St James of Compostella. The French word for shell is *coquille*. The director of the former Norwich bakers Ashworth and Pike Ltd. tells us:
'The coquille derives its flavour from a spice known as coriander.' *F. Geo. Ashworth – Broad Norfolk (1949)*

3. & 4. Norfolk dumplings, the edible sort, come in two varieties, 'floaters' ('swimmers' in the Fens) and 'sinkers'. The former are made from a ball of bread dough dropped into boiling water, the latter from a flour and suet mixture which is similarly treated, or perhaps steamed above boiling vegetables like suet duff. (See p. 23) The OED tells us that dumplings (or dumplins) are 'a kind of pudding...of paste or dough...originally attributed to Norfolk.' Hence the word is universally used to characterise a resident of these parts. Dumpling may be from Norse *dumpe* to drop suddenly.
'An esquire of Norfolk eats two pounds of dumplin every meal.' *Steele – The Tatler No. 19 (1709)*

5. Marsh samphire *(Salicornia europaea)* or samphire (pronounced 'samfer') is a maritime plant, a glasswort, which grows on the salt marshes of the north Norfolk coast and is often referred to as 'Norfolk asparagus'. Cooked and eaten in a similar way to globe artichoke, the vegetable has a delicate taste of the sea. Another local name for it is 'St Peter's cress', which betrays the French origin of the name, a corruption of *'herbe de Saint Pierre'*.

6. 'Hollow biscuits', 'Norfolk nobs' or 'Norfolk rusks' all describe a form of crispbread peculiar to Norfolk and Suffolk a reminder of our historical connections with the Low Countries and Scandinavia where such breads are also popular. Made from a basic bread dough and shaped like a scone, they are lightly baked, split open whilst still hot, re-baked and then allowed to cool to obtain their distinctive crisp texture. The hollow sound that results from a light tap on a hollow biscuit adequately explains the origins of its name.

29. Sounding Off

The Norfolk dialect not only contains distinctive words, alternative word formations and unique structures, it is also spoken with a distinctive accent. All the following words describe the sounds which habitually come out of a Norfolk mouth. Can you say how or what they are 'sounding off' about?

1. Drant
2. Blar(e)
3. Rattock
4. Mardling

Two ol' boys a-settin the world ta roights wi' a good ol' mardle!

Answers

1   Forby says that drant is a 'droning or drawling tone' and may be Anglo-Saxon in origin, whilst the OED says it is 'an onomatopoeic word after drawl, drone or rant, recorded from Scotland and East Anglia.

'Every one has heard of the Norfolk 'drant' or droning and drawling in speech.' *On Early English Pronunciation with special reference to Shakespeare and Chaucer - A J Ellis (1869-89)*

2.   'Blareing' (rhymes with barring) is the sound made by a Norfolk child crying, although the OED also attributes the word to the bellow of a calf and the sound of a trumpet. The word has a number of spellings, blar, blare, blah, bleah, all of which stem from the Middle Dutch/Low German *blaren*.

William Cowper (1731-1800), that anguished poet who found solace from his melancholia on the Norfolk coast at Happisburgh, gives us:

'Blaring oft, With one consent all dance their dams around.' *Odyssey x 499 - William Cowper (1791)*

3.   Forby quotes 'rattock' as a noun meaning 'a great noise' and as a verb 'to make a great noise', claiming that the word is an emphasis of 'racket'.

4.   'Mardle', or 'maudle' is a verb meaning 'to chat or gossip'; the word can also be used as a noun to describe a discussion as in: 'him an' me had a rare good ol' mardle.' Derived from the Old English *moedlan*, this quintessential Norfolk word has been much favoured by dialect authors as a title for their work or for themselves. Typical examples include Bob Malster's dialect dictionary, *The Mardler's Companion*, and E.R.Cooper's *Mardles from Suffolk*. Jonathan Mardle was the pen name of journalist Eric Fowler (1909-1981), who in 1949 edited a collection of letters discussing dialect submitted by readers of the Eastern Daily Press, and also produced his own study of dialect in 1973, both works being entitled *Broad Norfolk*.

Bibliography

Ayres, Brian (1994)   *Book of Norwich* English Heritage

Anstey, Christopher (1766)   *Bath Guide*

Baker, Sir Richard (1643)   *Chronicle of the Kings of England*

Baldry, George (1939)   *The Rabbit Skin Cap* Collins

Bathurst, Bella (1999)   *The Lighthouse Stevensons* Ted Smart

Bloomfield, Robert (1802)   *Rural Tales*

Borrow, George (1857)   *The Romany Rye*

Brewer, Rev. E. Cobham (1870)   *The Dictionary of Phrase and Fable* Classic Edition Galleypress

Billy Bluelight Pamphlet (1994) Woodforde's Brewery

British Almanac and Companion (1884)

Broad Norfolk (1949) Norfolk News Co. Ltd.

Buckland, Francis (1875)   *Report on the Fisheries of Norfolk*

Buckland, Francis (1882)   *Notes and Jottings from Animal Life*

Butcher, David (1979)   *The Driftermen* Tops'l Books

Butcher, David (1987)   *Following the Fishing* Tops'l Books

Chambers Twentieth Century Dictionary W.R.Chambers Ltd.

Chaucer, Geoffrey   *Canterbury Tales: The Reeve's Tale*

Cooke, W.H (1914)   *Eccles-next-the-Sea & The Erosion of the East Coast* Manuscript

Concise Oxford Dictionary of Quotations Oxford Univ. Press

Daily News November 12th 1880

Darroch, E., Taylor, B (1975)   *A Bibliography of Norfolk History* Univ. of East Anglia

Davies, G. C. (1883)   *Norfolk Broads and Rivers* Blackwood

Day, Francis (1880-1884)   *The Fishes of Gt. Britain & Ireland*

Edwards, W.F. (1983)   *St Benet's Abbey Norfolk* (St Benet's Abbey Com.of Management)

Ekwall, Eilert (1960)   *Concise Oxford Dictionary of English Place Names* Clarendon Press

Ewans, Martin (1992)   *The Battle for the Broads* Terence Dalton Ltd. Lavenham

Forby, Robert (1830)   *The Vocabulary of East Anglia* David & Charles Reprint

Forrest, A. J. (1949)   *Craft Vocabularies* Eastern Daily Press March 11 1949

Gillett, Rev. Edward (1862)   *The Song o' Sorlomun*   Lark's Press

Grapes, Sidney (1958)   *The Boy John Letters* Norfolk News Company

Hales, Jane (1969)   *The East Wind* Charles N Veal & Co Ltd.

Hales, Jane & Bennet, Wm (1971)   *Looking at Norfolk* George Reeve Ltd.

Higgins, David (1987)   *The Beachmen* Terence Dalton Ltd.

Jones, Alison (1992)   *The Wordsworth Dictionary of Saints* Wordsworth Reference

Kirkpatrick, John (1845)   *The History of the Religious Orders and Communities of Norwich*

Lambert, J. et al. (1960)   *The Making of the Broads* Royal Geographical Society Research Memoir No.3

Larwood, G. P., Funnell, B. M.(1970)   *The Geology of Norfolk* Geological Soc. of Norfolk

Lewis, Charles (1982)   *Pierhead Paintings: Ship Portraits from East Anglia* Norfolk Museums Service

Malster, R.(1974)   *Saved from the Sea* Terence Dalton Ltd.

Malster, R. (1999)   *The Mardler's Companion : A Dictionary of E Anglian Dialect* Malthouse Press Suffolk

Mardle, Jonathan (1973)   *Broad Norfolk* Wensum Books

Marshall, William (1787)   *The Rural Economy of Norfolk*

Martineau, Harriet (1833)   *Illustrations of Political Economy Part 1* Vanderput & Snoek v85

Mee, Arthur (1940)   *The King's England, Norfolk* Green Pastures and Still Waters

Nall, J.G. (1866)   *Yarmouth and Lowestoft*

Nash, Thomas (1599)   *In Praise of Red Herring*

North Norfolk News January 29 1998

Oxford English Dictionary Oxford University Press(1971)

Norwak, Mary (1988)   *A Taste of Norfolk* Jarrold & Sons

Pestell, R. (1986)   *Palling-A Village Shaped by the Sea* Poppyland Publishing

Pestell, R., Stannard, D. (1995)   *Eccles-Juxta-Mare: A Lost Village Discovered* Steeple Publishing

Rainbird Clarke, R. (1963)   *Grime's Graves Norfolk* HMSO

Ransome, Arthur (1936)   *Coot Club* Jonathan Cape

Ransome, Arthur (1940)   *The Big Six* Jonathan Cape

Ransome, Arthur (1988)   *Coots in the North & Other Stories* Jonathan Cape

Ray, John (1674)   *South & East Country Words Register of St. Benet's Abbey, Horning (Twelfth Century)*

Robinson, B., Rose, Edwin (1983)   *Norfolk Origins 2 Roads & Tracks* Poppyland Publishing

Roberts, Bob (1981   *Breeze For A Bargeman* Terence Dalton Ltd.

Rose, Edwin (1978)   *East Anglian Archaeology Report No 8* Norfolk Museums Service

Rider Haggard, Sir Henry (1888)   *Colonel Quaritch*

Spurdens, W. T. (1858)   *Third Supplementary Vol. to Forby's Vocabulary*

Stibbons, P.,Warren, M., Lee, K., (1983)*Crabs and Shannocks* Poppyland Publishing

Suffling, Ernest (1885)   *The Land of the Broads* Perry

Tusser, Thomas (1565)   *Five Hundred Points of Good Husbandry*

Walker, R.   *Where's That? (Guide to Norfolk Villages)* Petersen Publicity Ltd.

Way (1440)   *Notes of a medieval lexicon.*

Westwood, Jennifer (1989)   *Gothick Norfolk* Shire Publications Ltd.

White, Walter (1865)   *Eastern England: From the Thames to the Humber*

Williamson, Tom (1993)   *Origins of Norfolk*

Wright, Dr Joseph (1905)   *English Dialect Grammar*

Wright, Thomas (1857)   *Dictionary of Obsolete and Provincial English*

Young, Rachel (1976)   *Treasures of the Yarmouth Museums* Norfolk Museums Service